Eleanor Black is an award-winning journalist and first-time mother who drinks far too much coffee, though not at coffee group meetings. She has a Master of Creative Writing degree from the University of Auckland and several unfinished novels languishing in her cupboard, but this is her first book. She lives in Auckland with her husband Tim, son Micah and terrier Scout.

ELEANOR BLACK

Confessions
of a
Coffee Group
Dropout

ALLEN&UNWIN

Allen & Unwin
Sydney, Melbourne, Auckland, London

83 Alexander Street
Crows Nest NSW 2065
Australia
Phone: (61 2) 8425 0100
Fax: (61 2) 9906 2218
Email: info@allenandunwin.com
Web: www.allenandunwin.com

Cataloguing-in-Publication details are available
from the National Library of Australia
www.trove.nla.gov.au

ISBN 978 1 87750 506 5

Set in 10/16 pt Palatino by Post Pre-press Group, Australia
Text design by Christabella Designs

10 9 8 7 6 5 4 3 2 1

For Tim and Micah, who make mothering fun.
And for all new mothers everywhere . . .

Contents

1. Welcome to the jungle
And good luck!

You have probably just had a baby, or you are pregnant and about to embark on the grand adventure. Congratulations! For the most part, you are going to have a lot of fun. Children are hilarious, even very small ones. They are endlessly entertaining and interested in life, which makes them interesting. Most people won't tell you that.

Other mothers, when you break the good news, are more likely to start in with their war stories—the 32-hour labour; the scary and rare hospital complication; the lost struggle, no matter how little Kapiti ice cream passes across their lips and how many abdominal crunches they do, to lose the stomach pooch that hangs over the top of their jeans; the 14-month-old who whipped off her nappy and smeared poo all over her bedroom wall and had to be blasted with cold water, nuclear-detox style, before she'd stop.

Just what you want to hear about when you are still

coming to terms with the fact that you have recently acquired porn-star boobs.

Tell them you're about to welcome a boy into your home, and the response will often be, 'Ha, good luck!' It can be overwhelming, and incredibly dispiriting. Everyone likes an excuse to recount horror stories and demonstrate their expertise, so instead of telling them to shut the frick up and let you enjoy your moment, you might want to consider ignoring them. Or not. Whatever feels right for you. After all, pregnancy means you have to give up soft cheeses, raw fish, chilled sauvignon blanc and sleeping on your back—you shouldn't have to give up swearing as well.

You won't get a lot of reassurance from other quarters. The image of mothering most often presented in magazines and on television and by the other new mothers you meet is pretty and pink and totally under control. You have a problem, you identify an agreed solution, carry out said action, and you move on to the next freeze-frame moment of parental bliss. Simple. When you question this arrangement, and possibly even mention that at your house everyone cries of an evening, you are met with blank looks and polite laughter. You are led to believe that you are entirely alone in feeling this way, and even a little bit weird.

Sometimes it can feel that the entire world has got together, had a meeting and agreed to lie to you. Does that mother in the skinny jeans and swishy haircut *really* bake biscuits and clean the loo when her baby is sleeping? She doesn't slump on the sofa and watch the loser parade on *Jeremy Kyle* to boost her self-esteem, or fall into the dreamless, drooling sleep of the damned? Has the woman sitting next to you at your coffee circle really made educational flash cards for her three-month-old? That she actually uses? I'm going to take a stab at this and say, no, she too is watching trash television in her downtime and she should be ashamed of herself for suggesting otherwise.

Mothers can be very hard on each other, by criticising their compatriots' efforts in toilet-training or establishing a bedtime routine or, more subtly, by giving the impression that they find this mothering gig easy, and can't understand why you don't, too. It is an insidious form of one-upmanship and it is, in my opinion, really damaging. No-one can maintain that level of effort and attention while surviving on broken sleep and overly sweetened mugs of coffee. No-one. One day you are going to stumble, perhaps after a night of waking every two hours with a teething baby, when you have just enough energy to move the centre of mothering operations from the bed to the sofa. You will decide to forgo the bath, to let the baby wear the same singlet for another day, to forget about trying to entertain him with books and musical toys and to let him watch television instead. You will—gasp—not give him any tummy time. You will not tell any of the other mothers about this lapse. And you will feel like a steaming heap of cow manure.

You'll feel bad because you have been convinced in ways both subtle and blunt that it is your job to not only mother your child to the best of your ability, but to mother *perfectly*. That means making no mistakes, taking no short-cuts, accepting nothing but the utmost performance from yourself as defined not by you and your family but by your larger community—by that I mean *everyone* from your midwife, to the parenting expert *du jour*, to an impossibly poised celebrity mother in the pages of your go-to gossip mag, to some mummy blogger in cyberspace who may as well live on Pluto for all that she can help you.

A hundred years ago this particular mothering problem didn't exist. Mothers weren't fed a constant diet of stories in the media concerning evil mothers, overworked mothers, supermothers and sexy mothers. They weren't scared stiff by doom-and-gloom reports about foetal-development problems, cuckolded into buying fancy sterilising equipment for bottles, reprimanded for using disposable nappies, or convinced that if they didn't start educating their babies in the womb they would end up failing kindergarten. That's not to say the mothers of yesteryear didn't have their challenges, and I wouldn't for a moment want to be bringing up a child in the early twentieth century. However, I don't think they used up much psychic energy worrying about whether they were mothering *correctly*—not like we do today.

It must be said that this is, for the most part, a middle-class problem, and in many ways we are lucky to have the luxury of it. There are thousands of babies in New Zealand who never get tummy time, never get read to, don't enjoy a healthy diet, nor do their mothers have the skills or wherewithal to improve their lives, and that is a national tragedy. My son was a star at his local Plunket, in a disadvantaged part of Auckland, because he hit his milestones on time and was such a happy, well-nourished guy. He was unlike many of his peers, and I felt grateful each time we visited that I had the support necessary to give him a good start.

But this pressure to produce textbook children while living a sort of magazine-spread lifestyle is a serious issue. Women all over the country, from Whangaparaoa to Napier, Auckland to Wellington, Nelson to Dunedin, are struggling to cope, or struggling to maintain realistic standards in the face of a barrage of advice and expectation that is, at best, annoying and at worst dangerous.

Motherhood has been professionalised in recent years and standards are now ludicrously high. Partly this is because women are having children later in life, when they have already achieved in other arenas—they are used to setting themselves tasks and ticking them off. After they have reached their goal of getting pregnant, and have bought every nursery item on their must-have list, they quickly find that the predictable, controllable part of motherhood is a smaller portion of the whole than they expected. You don't get to decide when your baby arrives, or what sort of baby you are going to get (boy or girl, chilled or tense, sleeper or night owl), or what curve balls that baby is going to lob your way. You just have to muddle through. If you are coming to motherhood later in life, like so many women (the average age for having a first child in New Zealand is now 30) this can be really hard to accept.

I was 34 when I had my son and I didn't have a clue what I was really getting myself into. For nine months I wandered around in a hormone-drenched daze searching out mothers and their children, looking for reassurance. If *she* can do it,

I would think, marking a teen mum in cutoffs and sparkly tank top strolling the mall with her newborn, so can I. If the woman in the Pak 'n Save car park packing groceries into her SUV while four whooping children under five whirl around her legs can do it—*with a smile on her face*—I can do it. If charismatic dum-dums like Katie Price and Britney Spears can do it, with all the distractions of fame and infamy and those enormous bosoms, then I can do it.

It's true, women are gifted with the ability to carry and birth children, and a biological drive to protect and nurture them. The love part just happens—I love my son more than I could have ever imagined. I love spending time with him and making sure his needs are met and that he is happy. The happy bit is the best of all, because he is the chirpiest little cricket I have ever met. He is joy in a cuddly package that smells like fresh-cut grass and marshmallows. I could not have hoped for more. That's not the issue.

Mine was a borderline 'geriatric' pregnancy, my second after a devastating miscarriage. And it turned out to be a somewhat dramatic birth: my baby's blood pressure dipped with every contraction because the umbilical cord was wrapped around his neck. He was blue when he arrived. His fingernails looked like my father's the day he died, a fact that upsets me now but, thanks to miraculous pain-relieving drugs, I was not too worried then.

Besides, the birth was the least of it, as any mother will tell you with the glint of grim experience gleaming in her eye. It's what comes after the birth that blows your mind: the change in the way other people view you and treat you, the difference in your feelings about yourself, and your role in the world and your ability to contribute to it. Your choice to have a baby is political, like it or not, and every choice you make thereafter—to breastfeed or bottle-feed, to stay at home or work outside the home, to use disposable nappies or cloth nappies, and organic sustainable cotton baby clothes or whatever hand-me-downs someone happens to give you, to join a coffee group or to say, 'I'd rather spend the morning listening to the bozos next door working on their crapped-out cars, thanks'—says volumes about you and your world-view.

I cried when my husband left me alone with my son that first night in hospital. I could not bear the idea that this perfect little man, with his full head of black hair and cloudy blue eyes, would one day expire and leave this earth, like every one of us. It was inexplicable and terrible. I was also overwhelmed with the realisation—present throughout my pregnancy but now unavoidable and anchor-like in its weight and function—that whatever this baby needed in the night, whatever comfort, nutrition, love, reassurance he required, it would have to come from me. And that burden—a privilege to be sure, but a burden nonetheless—would be mine for the rest of my life. I couldn't sleep.

I am the kind of person who researches any situation in which I find myself, usually a matter of reading lots of books on the subject and trolling the internet until my eyes have gone square and I realise I have spent the last 45 minutes in some information superhighway rest stop catching up with the latest on the Kardashian sisters. Pregnancy, childbirth and infant care was no different. It's not that I didn't read a tonne of baby books, or become a member of babycenter.com so I could track my embryo's development, or read the complimentary copy of *Little Treasures* that was sent to me after I made the mistake of going to the Parent and Child Show, where I was presented with so many options for nappy bags, nappies, strollers and educational toys that I panicked. If it weren't for my friend Anne I might still be there, nervously weighing up the advantages of the moses basket versus the bassinet. I did all those things and they raised my anxiety and made me more confused.

Later, I pushed my baby around in the beating sun for months before another mother showed me how the sun canopy on his stroller worked. I dropped out of a coffee group when one of the other mothers told me off for giving my son bottled food. I attended a packed baby-sleep seminar when I knew full well that what I really needed to do was let him scream instead of bouncing out of bed like a blinking yo-yo to feed him four or five times a night. I joined a baby music group when my son was just three months old simply so I'd have a reason to shower and apply eyeshadow and get out of the house. And then I struggled to gather the oomph to actually go, because then I would have to make conversation and, you know, dance.

All the while I found myself astounded at the role other people feel entitled to take in the raising of someone else's—my—child. The unsolicited advice offered in the doctor's waiting room, the snide comparisons dropped into supposedly friendly conversations about activity gyms and breast pads—added to the fact that each honest mother I knew, when asked, admitted that she, too, had struggled and found the whole mummy-and-me universe bizarre—was bemusing.

That realisation didn't make my first months at home any easier—they were the hardest of my life and, honestly, I was afraid to ask for help for fear of looking like a bad mother. All I wanted to do was love and cherish my baby. Instead, I was consumed with worry, as well as being exhausted, hormonally challenged, and overwhelmed with the importance of my new job. Besides, whenever someone did try to help me, I was incredibly sensitive to any perceived criticism and drove them away with my frantic attempts to appear competent and in control. It was ridiculous, but also it's an all-too-common reaction to motherhood, I now understand.

I hardly remember my first winter at home with Micah, and in many ways that is a blessing. It was a peculiar time—I felt as if I had stepped into some parallel universe in which the smallest people were in charge and all the tired ladies with blurred edges were their unappreciated slaves. I wrote about it, though, and here is part of a blog I posted on the website I co-founded with my husband, pundit.co.nz, after one too many well-meaning people assumed I was having a ball at home with my tiny taskmaster, reading books and eating cheesecake and having facials and hour-long baths:

Do you love being a mother? Do you love it?

As a new mother I get asked this all the time. Usually I answer, 'Yes,' with the appropriate aw-shucks grin. But sometimes I tell the truth, which is rather more complicated.

I write this with an adorable four-month-old reclining in

my lap like a tiny Roman hedonist, pushing his fist into my face every now and then for me to kiss. It is mid-afternoon and I am yet to shower. My hair is lank and the cut I asked the stylist to rush through a few weeks ago (as baby sat in the corner) is not really doing the business. My nails are bitten to the quick, my skin is scaly, and I'm wearing a robe that smells of sour milk. If the meter man or Plunket nurse turned up I would be mortified.

I haven't slept properly since the third month of pregnancy, which means I haven't been fully rested for nearly a year and, yes, my brain is suffering as a result. Some days I feel like a crazy person and I'm pretty sure, given my interactions with innocent bystanders at the supermarket and dairy, that I come off as a nut-job, too. No, folks, today I'm not loving it.

That doesn't mean I don't love the little hedonist. He is fabulous, the best. But he also is the most intensive project I have ever undertaken. He makes my master's degree look like a cake walk, a joke. Losing twenty pounds of puppy fat through consistent, boring gym training and boring, sensible eating? Pah! Rehabilitating my knee following three operations, no problem.

As a goal-oriented person who takes great pleasure in a job well-done, it is a real challenge to wake up every morning and start afresh. There is no finish line for this one, no grades or centimetres lost by which to measure progress. Just me and the kid, hour after hour, day after day.

And that's cool. Nothing that comes easy is ever really that satisfying, etcetera, etcetera. I just wish people would stop pretending that baby-wrangling in any way resembles a soft-focus ad for toilet paper. Babies are cuter than anything in the world. Actually, let me rephrase that: your own baby is cuter than anything in the world. But they are not magical—the cuteness and cleverness and amazingness of your wee child is not enough to take away the fatigue, self-doubt, anxiety, and confusion of your day-to-day existence as a new parent.

So let's be honest about it, and stop beating ourselves up for not absolutely loving it every moment of every day.

Eighteen months later, I still haven't been back to the hairdresser. It's just one of those tasks that has fallen to the bottom of my to-do list, because it is not as pressing as dealing with a gale-force toddler tantrum, or taking the dog for a walk before he gnaws off his leg in frustration, or getting the car serviced. There are only so many hours in the day, and my hair has rocked the same style since I was twelve, so what does it matter? The truth is it doesn't. Nor does it matter that your house does not look like you think it should, or that your arms are jigglier than you expected, or that the only solids your baby will even consider eating at five months are cheap mass-produced custards.

All of this is to say that I understand that when you're in the trenches, stewing at your antenatal class while the educator witters on about the evils of epidurals and the other prospective mothers nod sagely about the pain distraction presented by a few chips of ice, you could do with a different perspective. You could also do with a large glass of sauvignon, but that is by the by. Consider this book your different perspective.

And if no-one else has mentioned it lately, let me say: You are doing a great job, however you choose to parent. I'm sure of it. I wish you nothing but luck, support and love. Salut!

Further reading

The New Zealand Pregnancy Book: A guide to pregnancy, birth and a baby's first three months 3rd edition by Sue Pullon and Cheryl Benn, Bridget Williams Books, 2008

Your Pregnancy Week by Week 6th edition by Glade B. Curtis and Judith Schuler, Da Capo Press, 2008

'The Modern Mummy: What's her problem?' by Sarah Barnett, *NZ Listener*, 27 March–2 April 2010

2. Why darling, you look amazing!

And other lies about pregnancy

It may seem impossible now, but soon pregnancy will be a distant memory. In a twinkle, these months will blur into a vague recollection of excited expectation, a pinch of worry, and, yes, some discomfort. As soon as you have a baby in your arms, your focus narrows in on a whole new set of concerns. When I sat down to write about pregnancy a year after the event, I had to refresh my memory by re-reading a blog post I wrote about it just before Micah was born:

This is a magical time. Really. I have to keep reminding myself, because my legs ache and my stomach is stretched as tight as a bongo drum and I can't sleep through the night anymore. But I am lucky to be seven-and-a-half months pregnant in the height of summer. I am lucky.

I was never one of those women who idealised pregnancy and motherhood. I figured it looked like a tough journey and one I was not ready to undertake until about eighteen months ago. I do not go gooey in baby stores, I do not sigh over French design pieces for the nursery, I do not think a $1000 cot will do a better job. I do not find the stories about beautiful women in pregnancy magazines aspirational. I do not enjoy reading about toilet training or sneaking vegetables onto your toddler's plate and can't imagine that I ever will. There are so many necessary evils associated with children.

I do like jeans and trainers for babies—I have a silly fascination for miniature items—and I do like baby toys. My baby is already the owner of a noise-making jungle activity kit which drives the dog bonkers and a classic wooden Noah's Ark which the dog is not allowed anywhere near.

I do not enjoy my body's transformation, impressive as it is. Some people find me adorable, others are repulsed. Some people stand back for me at doorways and smile palishly at me in public toilets, others look through me as though my fecundity were too embarrassing to contemplate.

Before I was pregnant I think I was one of the smilers. After all, pregnant women, no matter how ponderous and frowny, are working hard. They are growing extra limbs and extra brains and beautiful brooch-like sets of ribs and tiny beating hearts. They are sharing their blood and oxygen with another person. They are literally getting kicked in the guts every day. Whether I wanted to join their ranks, well that was a Big Question, and one to be considered fully later.

I had a miscarriage early last year and my view of pregnancy and procreation changed. No longer was it a bonus, a nice addition to a full life, a way of insuring my old age and keeping my baby-mad husband happy. It was an imperative. As I realised that the bleeding was not actually going to stop, that this little flicker of possibility was to be extinguished—and that the whole process would take five long, painful days—I finally understood why people spend tens of thousands of dollars and go through years of 'are we, aren't we?' agony for the privilege of holding their own baby in their arms.

Funny how losing the chance to meet someone the size of a lima bean can hurt so much. Funny how it took getting pregnant a second time to make the miscarriage alright. And yet I often think of that first baby—well, foetus to be accurate, I don't want to oversentimentalise—and wonder what might have been.

This time around, my pregnancy is cushioned by known facts. We are having a boy. He is of normal size and very active. He appears to have long legs. We chose an obstetrician rather than a midwife because I was nervous. So our baby gets scanned a lot. He was practising breathing last time we popped into her office. One time he yawned.

I walk into the baby's room every now and then to have a little play with the blankets, rattles and books we have accumulated. I sit in the chair and imagine how it will be when there is a squirmy, crying, needy little being in there. I still can't quite imagine taking control of the situation and being a mum.

And I look around at all the other pregnant women sweating their way across the mall car park, hissing at their partners in Baby City, fanning themselves in the doctors' waiting room, grimly making their way up the nappy aisle at the supermarket, and I think, gosh, aren't we lucky?—pundit. co.nz, February 2009

Waiting for a baby to arrive is like waiting for a bomb to explode. You are the bomb. You have a fixed time of detonation, but unless you are scheduled for a caesarian, you don't yet know what it is, so as your due date approaches the tension mounts.

This is when most women will attempt to plan for the uncontrollable event by controlling whatever baby-related stuff they can: they will go over their nursery checklist, finish reading their heavily highlighted copy of *What to Expect When You're Expecting*, pack the hospital bag, arrange for the dog to stay with someone else when labour begins, cook meals for the freezer, compile a phone list for spreading the joyful news, and clean like a demon seeking holy retribution.

At this point you probably won't feel like a precious vessel, if in fact you ever did. If this is the case, please don't feel bad. You are far from alone. Pregnancy is hard work. You may not enjoy the changes your body makes to accommodate another person, you may not feel well, you will almost certainly be more tired than you even imagined possible. Your skin may be blotchy, your hair an unappealing oil slick, your lower legs swollen little tree trunks. The image of the beautiful, bountiful pregnant woman wandering around barefooted in a floaty maxi-dress, humming to herself joyfully and caressing her distended mid-section is just that: an image. It is about as useful as the example set by Heidi Klum, who returns to supermodel form three days after giving birth, dons a pair of angel wings and some filmy lingerie and hits the Victoria's Secret runway. She has performed this trick four times and every time I am sure I can hear the suppressed screams of new mothers everywhere.

A woman writing on a popular New Zealand mothering forum drew a chorus of 'amen, sister' when she admitted she had lied about her uncomfortable pregnancy, the intense pain of childbirth—which she minimised—and how much bloody hard work it is to care for a newborn, when she returned to her antenatal class for a baby-show-and-tell, for fear of putting other women off. She had since revised her view, thinking it was better for expectant mothers to know what they are in for so they can go into it prepared, and so that they don't feel like loony tunes if pregnancy and early motherhood doesn't thrill them. Pregnancy was not, for this honest mum, a time of contented nesting. As she wrote on ohbaby.co.nz:

> I was so sick and so disappointed in myself for not being a radiant, glowing mama-to-be. I felt guilty for feeling like this when I knew others had a much harder time getting pregnant. I didn't admit this to many women at all.

If you were a conspiracy theorist you might think we all downplay the dark side of the pregnancy experience because we don't want to frighten other women, thereby saving them from our fate, or because we are disappointed and even embarrassed by our own pregnancy struggles. I think it is more to do with putting a brave face on it, because when pregnancy goes wrong, it can go spectacularly wrong. This is not to say that some women don't have glorious pregnancies, because they do. It's just that when the overwhelming portrayal of pregnancy presented to us at the outset is one of bliss and contentedness, it is disappointing to find yourself 'failing' to enjoy every precious moment and in fact, to be looking forward to the end of it.

For some, it can even be terrifying, as Jackie, a mother of two boys found:

I lost my first son at 33 weeks to strep B, an infection which is deadly to babies. So, as you can imagine, when I got pregnant the second time I spent the whole time worrying that I would lose this baby too. Fortunately, with the doctor's care and careful monitoring I ended up with two more beautiful healthy boys, but I never did pregnancy very well. With my eldest I got to 34 weeks before developing toxaemia and being hospitalised. The same thing happened with my youngest, putting us both at such risk that he was born by emergency caesarian and the doctors told me, 'No more babies.'

Such is the desire to have children that women will go to incredible lengths to deliver a healthy baby, even after many miscarriages and health scares, and sometimes many thousands of dollars in medical care. Is it any wonder that they approach pregnancy with trepidation and crossed fingers rather than jubilation and a flurry of excited emails? Maree, mother of two, describes her experience:

It took six pregnancies, 35 ultrasounds, a failed CVS [chorionic villus sampling—to detect birth defects] and amniocentesis for me to take a pregnancy to term. By the time my first son was born I had been pregnant for a total of 95 weeks—isn't that the same gestation as a whale?

I wrote an article in *Next* magazine in 2009 about an Auckland couple who spent three years and $200,000 trying to get pregnant. Happily, Bronwyn and Kelvin got their dream family—adorable twin daughters—but first they had to endure eight failed IUI (intrauterine insemination) procedures and two failed IVF (invitro fertilisation) treatments. They were diagnosed with 'unexplained infertility' but through a couple of pieces of luck made contact with a Chicago-based immunologist and obstetrician who believed Bronwyn's body was attacking Kelvin's cells. When they undertook his unproven treatment, Kelvin waged an heroic battle with local bureaucracy and international time zones that required him to stay up late into the night to make phone calls to the United States and to race around town collecting courier packs of chilled medication with a limited shelf life. They also had to fly to Sydney for blood treatment. The whole gruelling experience drained their bank account and their emotional reserves. 'The rest of your life is on hold,' Bronwyn told me. 'It's the hardest thing I've ever been through. We're fortunate enough not to find out what would have happened if we didn't get there.'

Like so many aspects of motherhood, the boring, uncomfortable and embarrassing parts of pregnancy tend to get glossed over. While the discovery that one is pregnant is usually joyful, the nine months that follow can be a dispiriting marathon. I think most people try to buoy up the pregnant woman's spirits by playing into the myth that pregnancy is this wondrous interlude in which you can eat like a long-haul trucker and expect people to wait on you. This just makes it hard for a woman to admit that she does not like it.

I was sick for the duration of my pregnancy. I never vomited, but I was constantly nauseous, with a nasty metallic flavour coating the back of my tongue that no amount of toothpaste or mouthwash could chase away. The only respite was sleep and we have some tragic photographs of me napping on the sofa in the middle of the day with the dog curled protectively at my shoulder like a fluffy gargoyle. I loathed my pregnancy wardrobe, discovering early on that cute maternity clothes cost a lot more than I was willing to spend on garments I would wear for only a few months. I made do with a few key pieces and regular clothes in bigger sizes, which is probably why my stomach peeped over the top of my trousers like a friendly dolphin. One of the few things that made me feel better was a daily bowl of two-minute noodles, preferably oriental flavour, something I hadn't eaten since university. All the while I kept a nervous eye on the bathroom scale because my doctor was firm: I should gain no more than twelve kilos during my pregnancy, including the water bloat that cruelly strikes you in the final weeks. More than that was unnecessary and unhealthy, she said. This was when I started to wonder if a delicate porcelain doll-like doctor was the best choice for me.

By the time I was at 39 weeks I was more than ready to meet my baby, and get my body back, although if you plan to breastfeed, your body won't truly be your own until the baby is weaned. Just a heads up.

The last two weeks at home were a weird little holiday. With the noodles and the bad attitude, it was like I had reverted to 1995. I listened to Nirvana and Nine Inch Nails and lay around watching junk on television, popping rice crackers in my mouth. I spent large chunks of time feeling sorry for myself and resentful towards my slim and energetic husband. Here, a log of my activities in those last days:

* After showing up at the wrong branch of an ultrasound franchise to find out the boy's weight and wasting everyone's time, I went for a coffee, taking advantage of the fact that I could still follow my whims. (Yes, I drank coffee occasionally in the late stages of my pregnancy. Maybe that's why my child has been such a dreadful sleeper.) I sat at a table next to two mums who spent 40 minutes talking about nappies while I ate an Afghan biscuit the size of a side plate and sadly contemplated a future in which I, too, would spend 40 minutes talking about nappies.

* I bought the dog a new collar embellished with 70s-style orange and brown stripes. He looked very handsome although when I fastened it round his neck he shook dramatically as if it were a snake.
* I watched Rachel Ray make three fatty, beige meals out of leftover ham and mug for the cameras and decided that if we were to meet in person we would not be friends.
* I kept vigilant watch over the front gate. Some of the neighbourhood children liked to open it and see if the dog would run out to play with them and I became the kind of tiresome person who hangs out the bedroom window and shrills, 'Leave the gate, please'.
* I watched Jeremy Kyle yell at under-educated British couples who went on telly to learn the results of DNA tests to sort out the parentage of their babies. And then I watched the couples yell at each other and their in-laws and the stolid security guards who came on stage to sort them out. And I laughed like a hyena.
* I researched the boy's star sign, a highly irregular move because I don't believe in horoscopes. I haven't since I was about twenty and decided I didn't like what I read about myself in *Linda Goodman's Love Signs*. I learned that the baby would be prone to headaches and sunstroke which made perfect sense given that the one thing missing from his hipster wardrobe was little sun hats.
* I became a mailbox-watcher, padding down to collect the mail as soon as it arrived, only to encounter bills which I then didn't open and left lying in piles to enrage my slim, energetic husband. Ha!

My point is, do what you need to do to get through your pregnancy. And don't spend a lot of time fretting about the birth, because eventually the hour will arrive, and there's not really a lot you can do to prepare for it.

I remember with absolute clarity my last day as a pregnant woman. Friends visited and we spent a hot, languid afternoon sitting on the deck eating date cake and green grapes. I was having the occasional contraction—I paused in conversation to grit my teeth—but there was no pattern to them. My stomach roiled as the baby kicked. I was incredibly uncomfortable but thought endless cups of sweet, milky tea would solve the problem. And another slice of date cake. A couple more grapes.

'You'll go on for days yet,' said the friend with two daughters.

'I better bloody not,' I replied.

That evening the contractions began in earnest. My mother brought out a stopwatch, a family heirloom she had retrieved from storage especially. It had last been used by my father to time her contractions when she had me. She began noting them on a piece of paper, then gave the watch and paper to Tim when it came to bedtime. He stayed up with me until about 2 am, when we decided it would be useful for one of us to get some sleep. He woke my mother. Meanwhile the dog was glued to my side, bearded face creased with concern. He was my constant companion that night.

By 5 am we could no longer discern a pattern: one contraction followed another, sure enough, but at intervals of eight minutes, five minutes, six minutes and durations of

30 seconds, 60 seconds, 45 seconds. The doctor had said not to phone until there was an established pattern of contractions five minutes apart and lasting for a minute. It felt as though that would never happen, that early labour was some cosmic joke. At 7.30 am I was desperate and Tim made the call. When the doctor said we could go to hospital I cried with relief.

There followed a slow slide down Remuera Rd in busy morning traffic. I wondered what the school children waiting at the bus stop thought of the sweaty, nervous woman writhing in the passenger seat of a silver family wagon. When we made it to the hospital the doctor took one look at me and suggested it might be sensible to help things along with drugs. While disappointed, I was also glad to be guided in this decision. It wasn't a productive labour, I was told, which seemed an accurate assessment of the situation. I hadn't slept in 36 hours and I was feeling about as strong and vibrant as a wet dishcloth. Time to get this job done . . .

I was sent to pace a quiet hall with stunning views of the city and harbour. Rangitoto was a scoop of ice cream floating in a pool of caramel sauce. Every time a contraction began I grabbed onto a window ledge and marvelled at the level of pain involved in getting a baby born—it was stupendous, truly life-altering, and I was just getting started. I watched hospital staff whipping around with clipboards, waited for Tim to return from parking the car on the far side of Jupiter, marked time until I could go and lie down . . . when would they let me lie down? I was so tired.

Finally, I was led to a room with more incredible views and the sweet relief of an epidural. And then, hours of waiting, hooked up to an IV, a baby monitor strapped around my abdomen. Tim dozed while I watched the midwife tracking a blue squiggled line on a roll of paper. The baby's blood pressure was falling each time there was a contraction. I knew this wasn't good but in my exhaustion, and perhaps due to the painkillers, I wasn't as alarmed as I might have been.

To pass the time, the midwife told me about her holiday in Africa. She had photographed the Big Five: I was entranced. I wanted to go. As soon as possible. I flip-flopped between euphoria and dread. The baby was coming! *Bugger, the baby was coming*. And I daydreamed about the birth I might be having if I were Scarlett O'Hara and Atlanta was burning around me, because *Gone With the Wind* is one of my favourite books. I have read it at least five times and each time I am reminded of being fourteen, when summer felt like it might last forever and I could fritter a whole day on the sofa with a thick book. But I have always been troubled by Scarlett's first birth, when her friends and family have already evacuated the Union Army-besieged Atlanta, and her hysterical young attendant offers to 'cut the pain' by slicing through the mattress with a knife. How wonderful to be in a clean, cool hospital with someone sensible to help me, I thought. How lucky I am.

Then the doctor returned to tell me it was time to push. I was numb from hip to toe, but I pushed for all I was worth and soon Micah, our little boy, arrived in a rush. He was purple from lack of oxygen, but his arms were reaching out for us. Perfection.

As a culture we have developed some really unhelpful attitudes toward pregnancy that lead pregnant women to believe it is some kind of consequences-free mini-break in Fiji. We are weirdly permissive—the all-you-can-eat mummy-buffet, the volcanic temper tantrums excused by hormones, the expected expectant woman's spending spree. But, we also have a tonne of rules pregnant women are supposed to follow—no soft cheese, no spa pools, no jumping on the trampoline, no raw fish, no hair dye, no drinking. The princess syndrome, in which everything revolves around the pregnant princess, clashes with the foetus-centric view that pregnancy is all about the baby. It is a strange contradiction and it can be confusing, especially if the woman carrying the child is the first of her close friends to have a baby, or is coming to it later in life, when she is used to doing what she wants, when she wants.

When I was pregnant I thought I would have a lot more fun than I actually did. Mostly because I'd watched pregnant women on sitcoms getting pandered to and assumed I would be, too. Yes, pregnancy is a special time—but it doesn't make you any more special than you were before you conceived. You may want to reconsider the 'Baby on Board' bumper sticker. Do you really think people are going to drive differently in your presence because you have one of those? *Seriously?*

Here are my top eight pregnancy myths:

1: You can eat as much as you like when you're pregnant
Oh, that this were true, because you will be as hungry as a marauding rhino and your instinct will be to shove whatever food-like substance you can grasp into your gaping mouth. There are two major problems with this. First, not all foods are created equal and you must ensure that you are eating the fruits, vegetables, proteins and healthy starches that will provide essential nutrients to your developing baby. Unfortunately, you will crave a load of salty, fatty, sweet junk and avoiding said junk will be a daily struggle. Secondly, there is no Get-Out-of-Jail-Free card in this game. Every kilo that you gain while pregnant has to be shifted once the baby is born. It doesn't just fall off, regardless of what Heidi Klum might imply, the Bavarian pixie. The healthy range for pregnancy weight gain is roughly 8–20 kilograms. You will lose about five kilos when the baby is born. The rest you are going to have to shift yourself. Sure, you will shed some weight as you burn calories breastfeeding, but in my experience this process wasn't as miraculous as I had been led to believe. When breastfeeding finished I still hadn't returned to my pre-pregnancy form and I probably never will.

2: You will adore your baby bump
Your attitude to the bump will change over time. In the first months of pregnancy, when you feel like a sack of rotten potatoes but have nothing to show for it, you will be desperate to develop a baby bump, something to pat speculatively when you

are browsing the glossy mags in the supermarket checkout, and something to point in your partner's direction when he is being a pain. A baby bump can be a quick equaliser in any argument you are too tired to wage. You'll photograph the bump and buy a couple of new pairs of pants that expand around it. Then your bump will grow . . . and grow . . . and grow. Your skin will feel weirdly stretched and just when you think it couldn't possibly accommodate more bump, you'll grow some more. Eventually, your bump will move on its own, when the baby kicks, and you'll love it again: 'It's a miracle! Did you feel that?' And by the time you are 38 weeks plus, and your bump is a heavy, hot mass that puts strain on your back and legs, you'll want rid of it. You might even daydream about pulling it off and leaving it under a beach umbrella while you take a quick dip.

3: Books about pregnancy are helpful and you should read as many as you can

Books about pregnancy are, as a rule, *not* helpful. They will dazzle and terrify you with demoralising lists of the things that can go wrong, a bunch of don'ts and do's, and they will turn you into a jangling mass of nerves. Sometimes being forewarned is not being forearmed. When you are pregnant you are incredibly vulnerable to the suggestion that something bad might happen to your baby. Why put yourself through it? Listen to everything your healthcare provider tells you, pay attention to your body, and leave it at that. If you must read a book about pregnancy, try *Operating Instructions: A Journal of My Son's First Year* by Anne Lamott, *The Girlfriends' Guide to Pregnancy* by Vicki Iovine, or *Mommies Who Drink: Sex, Drugs and Other Distant Memories of an Ordinary Mom* by Brett Pae-sel. At all costs, avoid *A Life's Work: On Becoming a Mother* by Rachel Cusk. It is a beautiful book, but should only be read when you are in tip-top psychological shape.

4: You can achieve the fashionable pregnancy look sported by celebrities

You can't, so forget it. Save your energy for something achievable, like finishing *War and Peace*, or de-cluttering the house. As we all know, celebrities are not like you and me. They have access to funds, staff and fabulous clothing that we don't. Halle Berry, Gwen Stefani, Naomi Watts, Rachel Weisz—they all have more help than you do, and they have cuter handbags. Deal with it. Getting yourself dressed and out of the house should be your only sartorial goal during pregnancy. Truly, it's an accomplishment and you deserve a round of applause. Go you!

5: You will get special treatment

As soon as your bump appears, people will hold doors open for you, offer you preferential treatment at restaurants and petrol stations, and give up their seats on the bus for you. Right? Um, no. Not unless they are men over the age of 60 because chivalry is dead, my friends, and good manners are pretty much extinct as well. Okay, that was harsh—there are some thoughtful folks out there who will see your situation and do whatever small thing they can to make it easier for you, be it carrying your supermarket shopping to your car or bending down to pick up the change that fell out of your wallet when you were fishing for your cash card. But most people don't give a rat's arse.

6: Pregnant women have a lot in common

Um, that they are reproductive females? This is kind of like saying that all Jewish people get along with each other, or that all redheads are friends. Just because you are in an antenatal class together, doesn't mean you will bond for life. True, it's a great icebreaker but you can only talk about babies for so long before you tire of yourself, or other people start shooting imaginary poisoned darts at you. You might make a bunch of mummy friends while pregnant, and that's wonderful if you do, but don't feel like a loser if you don't.

7: You will be rewarded with diamonds

This happens on television and in movies all the time, and occasionally you read about some C-list celebrity like Tori Spelling who is given a sparkling chunk of carbon to mark the birth of her child. Closer to home, I heard of a real-live Auckland woman who was presented with 'two carats, one for each ear' when she had her third child. News presenters seem to have a trend for diamond-encrusted letters worn around the neck to represent each child's name and designers and stylists (or at least those featured in design magazines) tend to favour stackable rings in different colours for each child. I have always thought this 'have a baby, get a diamond' tradition sounded charming and provided an excellent excuse to razzle-dazzle the jewellery box. However, in real life, out here in the suburbs and small towns and on lifestyle blocks throughout New Zealand, women who give birth are more often rewarded with a new washing machine or clothes dryer, or if very lucky, a morning at a day spa and a box of chocolates. For my own part, while hooked up to a foetal monitor and IV drip in the birthing suite, pale as parchment and woozy with exhaustion, I was promised an eternity ring. I think Tim felt bad for getting me into that predicament and knew the idea of something shiny and pretty would cheer me up, which it did for a few seconds. My ring hasn't materialised yet—babies and renovations suck up funds at an alarming rate—but I do have a lovely new kitchen bench.

8: You will bounce back

You might. Some lucky women do. After a couple of months of adjustment, a very few mothers report feeling 'better than ever' and even claim to weigh less after giving birth than they did before they were pregnant. One of these women is actually my friend, but she's a biological anomaly and a personal trainer. Most women—especially those over the age of 30—will not bounce back from pregnancy like a red rubber ball from a Christmas cracker. They will slowly claw their way back to something approaching normal after many months or, possibly even, several years. Lack of sleep is a major factor in your ability to feel good and on top of things. Take away a woman's unbroken sleep and she is forced to consume more food for energy, often in the form of sugary foods and drinks with excess calories and caffeine that do nothing to help her lose the weight gained in pregnancy. That also makes it much harder for her to muster the enthusiasm for exercise. Plus, mums don't have a lot of time to look after themselves and that, too, makes it tough to bounce back.

Pregnancy is a highly individual experience and you mustn't feel bad if yours doesn't conform to your ideal. In fact, you're better off not even imagining an ideal pregnancy because you are courting disappointment. Some pregnant women love it, others merely tolerate it. It doesn't actually matter which category you fall into, your baby will be fine. Like the whole mothering experience, pregnancy has been fetishised by people trying to sell you maternity jeans, souped-up bras, pregnancy magazines, aromatherapy candles, baby-friendly handbags that you could lug a miniature horse in, and special oils and potions to rub on your baby bump. Don't fall for it. If it makes you feel better, by all means buy it. But odds are you don't need it and after your baby has arrived you'll never want to see it again. Save your money—children are expensive.

The basics remain: eat well, sleep lots and don't expect too much of yourself. Enjoy whatever peace and serenity you can find, because soon you will have your hands full.

Further reading

Mommies Who Drink: Sex, Drugs and Other Distant Memories of an Ordinary Mom by Brett Paesel, Warner Books, 2006

A Life's Work: On Becoming a Mother by Rachel Cusk, Picador 2001

The Girlfriends' Guide to Pregnancy: Or Everything Your Doctor Won't Tell You by Vicki Iovine, Pocket Books, 1995

Operating Instructions: A Journal of My Son's First Year by Anne Lamott, Pantheon, 1993

3. Advice you may want to ignore

Antenatal class, mothers in the news, and 'helpful' strangers

We ended up in our third-choice antenatal class. The one associated with the hospital filled up months before I even thought to get on the waiting list. The other popular class for expectant parents in our area was expensive, and in those last, dwindling pre-baby days we were saving hard to prepare for losing my income. And so it was that we spent six miserable Tuesday evenings in the peak of the summer heat in a sticky church hall—with no air-conditioning, or electric fans, or even enough windows—watching ouchy birthing videos shot in West Auckland in the early 90s and playing silly word games with no discernible subject or object. We burgeoning mothers looked like a collection of sweating Christmas puddings plopped on plastic chairs to cool before serving. Glowing? I don't think so—more like oozing.

Our instructor was a well-meaning former midwife who

maintained a beatific and, to my mind, wholly unrealistic stance: childbirth was a magical, fairies-dancing-in-the-back-garden occurrence; contractions didn't hurt—they were 'strong'; medical intervention into the birthing experience was 'bad'; and breastfeeding was the most wonderful, fulfilling experience on this earth. For the daughter of an orthopaedic surgeon and an intensive-care nurse, whose view of the medical profession had always been one of profound gratitude—and who fully intended to accept any pain relief and/ or doctor's advice offered during labour, thanks very much— our instructor's stance was alienating.

But then, I had already chosen an obstetrician as my lead maternity carer (LMC), a decision that marked me apart. According to a longitudinal study based at the University of Auckland, *Growing Up in New Zealand*, about two thirds of expectant mothers in New Zealand choose an independent midwife as their LMC, with hospital-based midwives the next most popular choice. In certain mummy circles choosing an obstetrician as your LMC is a no-no, because 'doctors want to take the power away from women, and medicalise their birthing experience'. I find this nugget very difficult to swallow and my own view is that the overwhelming majority of doctors (because like any profession, there are some less than fabulous practitioners out there) are committed to mothers' health and want to avoid what used to be a common, tragic occurrence: the death of a woman during or soon after childbirth. Mothers who choose midwives as their LMCs are supported to do so, and I reckon mothers who choose a doctor should get the same support—or at least not feel embarrassed every time the subject comes up, which is often when you are pregnant.

Like any class, there were stock figures who emerged from the group. The class clown was a well-to-do, older dad who wore boat shoes sans socks and insisted on making jokes about episiotomy tears and Lamaze breathing. Every freaking class, ha-ha! An earnest and clearly terrified woman with a blokey, she'll-be-right partner who liked to jeer at her concerns for the entertainment of the group, asked endless questions about birth: Could the epidural really paralyse her? What if the baby got stuck? Did the use of forceps result in a cone-head baby? I was mocked for taking notes in a little book with butterflies on the cover. Backtrack twenty years and I could have been sitting in fifth-form English, being mocked for owning a Jemima Puddleduck pencil case and taking notes about the life of war poet Wilfred Owen, not an experience I had ever hoped to recreate.

I don't remember much of what we learned at our antenatal class although I won't soon forget the absurdity of watching eight or ten men standing at a long trestle table struggling to fasten cloth nappies on slippery plastic baby dolls. It was like something out of a fatherhood guidebook from 1953 . . . 'Supportive fathers like to learn some of Mother's jobs.' It got worse when the men were sequestered in a room to brainstorm clever ways with mince while the women practised pelvic floor exercises. As Tim pointed out, he is the cook in our household and he perfected his mince recipes decades ago.

What really stands out for me, though, is the fringe stuff we learned that could only be useful to a tiny portion of the population and, therefore, in my opinion, really didn't belong in a mainstream antenatal class. For example, there is a group of mothers in Nelson who never let a nappy touch their babies' bums, but carry buckets around for them to pee and poop into. They do this because it is environmentally friendly and because they reckon it strengthens the mother-child bond, surely something to be celebrated, but it seems a little extreme to me. Anyway, I was so intrigued I looked them up online and, sure enough, there they were leading a workshop with babies peeing into buckets on cue. This was something for us to consider, said our instructor.

She also told us about the 'lotus birth' movement in which women allow the placenta and umbilical cord to dry out and fall off naturally after birth, a process that usually takes two to three days but can take up to a week. Some women even sew a little velvet pouch for it to rest in and apply salt and lavender oil to deal with the smell. The idea is that the placenta continues to provide the baby with energy after birth, and that it can be traumatic to the infant for the cord to be cut before it has had a chance to 'say goodbye'.

'Not true,' said my obstetrician when I asked about whether babies have an emotional bond with the placenta. 'Once the baby is born, the placenta's job is done.' She was too horrified and I was too embarrassed to discuss it further.

The antenatal class 'graduation' celebration was held at a bar close to the church hall. The fathers gratefully swigged pints and the mothers resentfully sipped glasses of orange juice and soda water, except for one brave woman, days away from her scheduled c-section, who ordered chardonnay and was never heard of again. We had to shout to be heard above the noise. 'We must do this again' was yelled over and over in an entirely hollow fashion that really meant, 'I wish you no harm, but would rather not see you after this'.

A few of the mothers did meet a couple of times afterwards, and attempted to get to know each other as we peered over the tops of enormous coffees, worked our way through brick-like caramel slices and held up wrinkled babies dressed in their best little jeans and beanies. Then the emails dried up and, presumably, most of the women returned to work. I stayed at home and lost my mind, but more on that later.

My doubts about the usefulness of antenatal classes are not uncommon. I have a friend who refused to even consider attending them after hearing too many unsettling stories. And Andrea, mother of one, told me:

Spending eight weeks learning about how to go into labour is a waste of time—new mothers need more information to help them *after* the birth.

___

The first time I realised that other people's perceptions of my mothering would matter to me was two weeks after my son's birth. We were on a family outing at the garden centre. My husband was set on planting a vegetable garden in a sad little patch of our yard where a tree had died. I was just happy to be out of the house breathing some new air, and Micah was perfectly himself: content to be with his parents, gazing fuzzily at punnets of lettuce and spring onions. I recall feeling secretly prideful of our family tableau—wholesome vegetable-buying father, tired but attentive mother with good hair, adorable baby. We were iconic, like the holy family, or the Pitt-Jolie family. Enviable. Well, you know pride always precedes a fall and mother-pride precedes a big ol' reality check.

It was a glorious late-autumn day and we had become intoxicated with the idea of our lovely life-giving garden, piling our cart with punnets of silver beet, tomatoes, radishes, carrots, pumpkins and beans. Micah was lying in his pram, blanket tucked under his feet and around his torso, one arm defiantly stuck out of the cocoon. (Even in his ultrasound photo, this kid had one fist raised as if to say, I may be small but I set my own agenda. Peace, hombres.) Tim had asked the incredibly helpful garden-centre lady about insect-deterring plants, and she duly pointed us towards yellow and orange marigolds we could scatter between the veges like edible bursts of sunshine, when she turned to me and dropped a bomb. 'What a beautiful baby,' she said as I purred with pleasure at the compliment. 'Shouldn't he be wearing a hat?'

I felt like I had been slapped. 'Oh, he has a whole bunch of hats at home. I thought I, um, had one in the nappy bag,' I blathered, scrabbling through the nappy bag and coming up with an extra dummy (was that a judgmental raised eyebrow from the garden-centre lady?) and some tiny socks. 'Knew I'd forget something!' My crooked smile was ignored and the helpful garden-centre lady went to improve someone else's day. I took her criticism to heart and nursed it like my neglected baby.

Why do we do this to each other? It is a terrible contra-diction that while we seem to be quite comfortable to chime in when we see a perfectly happy baby on an outing minus one not-necessarily vital layer of clothing, we don't speak up when children really need our help. Every week small chil-dren turn up at hospital because someone who was supposed to be looking after them chose to hurt them instead. Certainly it is easier to point out the perceived evils of formula-feeding than to say to an adult that they are mistreating a child, or to pick up the phone and call the appropriate social service when something is seriously wrong. But that is the topic for another book, and here we are talking about different pressures.

As Nikki, who had her first child at 30, said, the number one thing that would make mothering an easier job is for people to keep their opinions to themselves when advice is not asked for. After all, a mother's harshest critic is almost always herself. Really and truly. A common theme with women I sur-veyed for this book was feeling bad about not being a perfect mother, as defined by magazines, books, television images, newspapers, parenting classes and other mothers. Bronwyn, a mother of two, was particularly articulate on this point:

I don't believe in full-time childcare, so I have my kids at home (apart from a few creche sessions a week). But I work, for the sake of my sanity and pride as well as the family finances—sometimes up to 20 or 30 hours a week.

And I feel I should use cloth nappies (for the envi-ronment), feed my children fresh organic food (for their health) and dress them in expensive New Zealand merino and organic cotton (for their health and the environment). I feel bad every time the almost-three-year-old sits in front of the television, and I'm constantly berating myself for not spending more time kicking a ball with him, or teaching him how to count, or baking cupcakes with him. I feel bad that he doesn't know his nursery rhymes when the other kids can recite the entire Mother Goose Compendium.

I feel bad if I realise at the end of the day that I haven't offered him enough water to drink, or enough fruit to eat. I feel bad if I let a sniffle develop into a full-blown cold. I feel bad if we have takeaways too often for dinner. I worry that the baby is not being turned upside down enough—good for their mental development, apparently—and I'm not doing enough to give him a stimulating environment. I feel bad if I let the baby cry himself to sleep or lose patience with the toddler. I feel that I should be able to keep my house tidier than it is, and that our routine should be more orderly. I feel that I should be doing more exercise and I shouldn't be spending as much time on the internet . . .

None of this is direct external pressure; it's all coming from me. I get—I admit it—a little obsessed with this image of what a perfect mother should be.

I long ago gave up on the idea of attaining anything approaching mothering perfection because, frankly, it was never within my reach, but I do, at least, try to look competent.

My son sometimes works against me. When he was about four-teen months old, Micah learned how to silently slide out the dog door we had installed in the lounge to let our highly excit-able terrier, Scout, come and go. In this way, both Scout and Micah could easily access the garden by way of a low deck with no railing. He did it with great care but, for the first two months or so, I ran out into the garden squealing every time. Then his toddler's irrepressible single-mindedness wore me down and I ran out of energy. He was in a fully fenced yard, I reasoned, and the dog was with him. His balance was also surprisingly good.

Not long after we moved into our new house, I was taking dog and toddler for a walk when I found out that our neigh-bours had been watching this little bit of theatre with concern for some weeks. The very sweet man from next door stopped me to ask how 'the little darling' was doing. 'We've seen him, on the deck by himself,' he reported. 'My wife said, "If the mother doesn't come out soon I am going over the fence!"' Given that she is very demure and can often be seen adjusting her hijab as she pops outside to hang out the washing, this was an image with great appeal. 'That's something I'd like to see,' I thought, although obviously the shame would be acrid.

'I know,' I told our neighbour, 'we are trying to teach him not to use the dog door, but it's hard. He sees the dog do it, and he loves the dog and mimics him all the time. He just wants to be like Scout.'

This cut no ice with our neighbour and a few weeks later I found an admonishing newspaper clipping in our mailbox. The headline declared 'Cat-flap kid's amazing adventure' and it was a *Sunday Star-Times* story about a cherub-cheeked two year-old who crawled through the cat door at his grand-parents' house on Auckland's North Shore and made it all the way to the beach, more than a kilometre away. When a group of children found him an hour later, he was soaking wet. 'Cold,' he said. 'Scared.' 'Rocks.'

Micah didn't know any of those words yet, so I guessed we would be saved that indignity. I stuck the clipping on our fridge for a few weeks as a reminder of the level of attention and care our neighbours direct at us, making a mental note to keep on top of the pruning, then I moved it into the office, where it sat on a stack of papers for a while. Now it's gone, lost in the tumult of our home, but its warning is burned into my conscience.

The wonderful thing about this information age is that not only can we measure ourselves against the advice we receive from Plunket, the Ministry of Health, the midwife, the doctor, various media-friendly childcare experts, our own parents, siblings, and every other parent or prospective parent we know—we can measure ourselves against total strangers living many thousands of kilometres away.

Like many women, Lee-Anne, mother of two, got a taste of this early on:

> When Ruby was a baby I was getting weekly email updates from babycentre.co.uk but they were dread-ful. Basically they made me feel that if my baby hadn't

completed her PhD by the time she was five weeks old I was failing. Okay, actually it was things like, 'Your baby may be able to push himself up on his arms and do mini push-ups.' Ah, no, no, she can't. Oh, God! She's an imbecile! Yeah, I unsubscribed. They made me feel that if my baby wasn't doing what it 'should' be doing, clearly I was doing something wrong.

My weekly internet trawls to check on what's new in the mothering realm always throw up some factoid or 'parenting expert' I'd rather not know about:

* British research finds working mothers are even further behind in the pay stakes than realised.
* Ten-year-old Romanian girl gives birth.
* More ordinary mothers are getting tummy tucks and breast jobs to maintain their pre-baby looks.
* Six per cent of Kiwi mums have to use IVF to get pregnant.
* The Duggar family from Arkansas have nineteen children ('and counting!' as they declare on their website). In related news, the Duggar family have a reality TV show.
* There is a new mummy battle brewing, between perfectionist 'Stepford Mums' aged under 35 and 'Midlife Mums' in their 40s who say they are more laid back in their parenting style. (There are blogs about this last phenomenon, and newspaper articles, and t-shirts. I had no idea.)

In the United States there is a blogger with *Little House on the Prairie* corkscrew curls, two children, a 'wonderfully supportive husband' and a gun licence. She thinks all families have the responsibility and the right to protect themselves with firearms. She also thinks vaccination programmes might be some kind of bizarre plot concocted by the medical establishment to give children autism—because we all know doctors and nurses are as bad as the KGB. Plus she home schools, which means her children are doomed to get only her side of the story until they hit majority. Now, clearly I could choose to ignore this woman, but since I've known she's out there I have felt compelled to check in on her every once in a while to see what kind of damage she might be doing.

There are endless money-saving tips shared by mums online, an indicator of the dire state of our economy and the back-to-the-future trend for families to live on one income while the children are small. Some of these tips are very good, but some of them involve cutting coupons and organising them in plastic folders to buy products you wouldn't ordinarily use simply because they cost 30 cents less. Others require you to spend many hours online searching for products you may or may not actually want in the hope of earning (within a month or two) a five-dollar voucher from Amazon or a similar website. Forgive me if I contain my excitement.

I enjoy those parenting-themed websites with an irreverent sense of humour and a focus on domestic harmony. I can fritter hours—and have—on younghouselove.com, stealing ideas for cheaply improving Micah's bedroom and taking better photos of him. Prudentbaby.com has instructions for making chic makeup bags, totes and sundresses for next to nothing, if you are so inclined, and makeitlovely.com is good for party tricks: you, too, can thrill your two-year-old with a rainbow cake and matching bunting.

When Micah was about six months old, I was surprised to learn (online, of course) that mummy blogging as a social trend was passé, although some days I splash around in the comforting snark of coolmom.com as if my life depended on it. Apparently, it is no longer enough to share with all and sundry that you spent the morning cleaning spit-up off three dozen organic-cotton bibs and performed a puppet show about the giant turtles of the Galapagos Islands, and expect people to be impressed. Now, if you want to be a trendy, right-on mummy you post your birth online. There really is such a thing as too much information, and this is it.

A woman from California told the *New York Times* that she found these films very helpful, and was so moved when she watched some German guy rub his partner's back during labour that she cried. I nearly cried, too, when subjected to birthing videos at our antenatal class—from embarrassment and suppressed mirth. Firstly, a birth is an incredibly intimate experience and seeing strangers go through it, while surrounded by virtual strangers in an airless church hall decorated with posters of the birth canal, made my cheeks flame. Secondly, all official birth videos used for sex-ed and birthing classes were shot sometime between 1972 and 1993—the fashions are hilarious.

Watching an Auckland couple circa-1990 welcoming their second child into the world at their home was, admittedly, a memorable experience. But it wasn't that I picked up tips for my own childbirth so much as it developed an even stronger preference on my part for painkillers and privacy. The image of the couple's older child toddling in to the bedroom to check on proceedings and the father's colour-block jersey and gigantic eyeglasses will take years to expunge. Not to mention the family portrait shot minutes after the birth, when the mother pulled the baby and attached umbilical cord from between her legs for some impromptu memory-making. Admittedly, I have never been a let-it-all-hang-out kinda gal. But every person who has heard about the umbilical-cord portrait was surprised, and not in a gee-that's-cool way.

As far as instruction goes, really I don't think there's anything that can prepare you for childbirth. It's a hell of a way to spend a day and thank goodness you don't have to do it on a weekly basis. Enough said. The ad nauseam dissection of labour-day plans and the birthing-pool tips provided by Carla from Kansas aren't really going to help you with your own birth experience.

Besides, our ancestors managed to do it—once a year, some of them—without the aid of any tech-savvy American chicks. My great-grandmother gave birth in a wooden shack in Paraguay multiple times, for goodness sake. Once, I'm told, with a jaguar perched in a tree above her. She also had to deal with a snake that coiled itself around her sleeping son and suckled from his bottle, an event witnessed by my grandmother—her eldest child and mother's help. So, I think I can imagine Eleanor McQuire Delugar's reaction to an online birthing vid—and it wouldn't have been to set up a camera at the foot of the bed.

I am starting to make my peace with the village that is helping me raise my boy. By this I don't mean extended family and friends, but the rest of the country. New Zealanders are a lovely, well-meaning bunch of people who, every now and then, deem it necessary to pitch in when they think I am not paying enough attention to my child. I say 'starting' because a large part of me, the part that used to listen to Hole, wear six coats of nail varnish and drink a six-pack of Diet Coke every day—and thankfully hasn't been seen since the late 90s— thinks they should mind their own damn business. But the better part of me, the part that married a nice man, got a dog and moved to the suburbs, appreciates their concern. Still, it is embarrassing to be pulled up on your mistakes, especially when they may impact your child. As Shan, mother of two, says:

At the supermarket, when my first was about six months old, a silly woman said, 'You know, you are over-feeding that child,' tutting and shaking her head. It was the morning after a bad night of sheet changes and mopping up puddles of baby sick more than once. I swore at her and told her to mind her own business. Then went to my car and cried.

I have a habit of coming to grief at cafes. When Micah was about nine months old we took him to Gisborne for a summer holiday, which also involved painting the interior of the 100-year-old farmhouse where my father grew up. As Micah hadn't yet got the hang of crawling, we popped him in an empty blow-up paddling pool we'd set up in the dining room with some toys and books, and talked to him as we painted. I would be up on the scaffolding working on the trim, Tim would be rollering the walls, the dog would be squealing at the possums living under the verandah, and Micah would be howling in frustration. Oh, and it was over 30 degrees every day. I don't know what we were thinking.

That is background, so you can understand how excited I was to get out of the house and meet a friend for coffee. We snagged a big table outside one of Gisborne's growing crop of effortlessly funky cafes and Micah sat on my lap, wiggling his toes in the breeze. My latte had just arrived at the table and, as I was reaching out to move it away from Micah, he grabbed it with that crazy strength babies have and spilled the whole lot over himself. Catastrophe. I froze. I knew about how susceptible babies are to burns, how a cup of liquid that is a comfortable temperature for an adult to drink can scald a small child horribly. I had written a magazine article about it, for pity's sake. I was a bad mother. Bad.

As my friend rushed to the kitchen to get a pitcher of ice water and a towel to wrap around Micah's abdomen, a woman from another table ran over and threw her glass of water on him. This snapped me to attention and I was able to peel off his clothes and take a look at him. He was pink, but no blisters, no real damage. He was okay and I was okay, but what a *filthy* look I got from the people at the next table. I deserved it without a doubt, but it took me some time to collect myself and not want to march over and explain that usually I was a *much* better mother than evidence might suggest.

The other day I met another friend at a waterside cafe in Auckland and spent the lunch hour trying to convince Micah that hanging his head out the window of the multi-coloured plastic playhouse set up conveniently next to our table was far more fun than picking up pebbles from the courtyard and throwing them at birds. His response? 'No! No no no. Nooo!' As my friend and I sat with our after-lunch coffees, Micah headed for the exit and into the adjacent park, where a giant fountain was calling his name. He did the toddler run—arms thrown out to the sides, head down like a Spanish bull, little legs pumping for glory. I really didn't think he'd go far. Besides, I was knackered and had not paid my friend the attention she deserved. She had a new job! There was gossip to be gathered!

I could see him clearly through the slatted fence, but I wasn't bargaining on the seagulls on the other side of the exit— plump, aggressive ones that were stealing picnic leftovers from an older earth mother with a plait down her back and her son. Micah was entranced, giggling and waving his arms at the seagulls, making small Spanish bull-style charges at them. Unlike other toddlers who always like to keep their mummies in view, he is confident to a dangerous degree. Nothing bad has ever happened to him and he expects this lucky state of affairs to continue, a philosophy he shares with our dog. He kept running . . . and running. Finally I got up and ran, too, scooping him up metres from the water hazard and the disapproving mum with the plait, who looked up at me expectantly.

'I thought he'd come back . . . eventually,' I explained, lamely and reluctantly, because, after all, I had kept him out of harm's way, hadn't I?

'Not with those seagulls around, he wouldn't,' she replied.

I swallowed my pride, put my boy under my arm, and returned to my table. There was no moral victory to be had, he wasn't even wearing a hat for jiminy's sake. Bad mother, me.

When I went to pay for my lunch the server, a young English man with an impeccably white set of teeth, laughed at me.

'You have your hands full there,' he said kindly. 'He'll keep you fit.'

'Yeah, he's always on the move!' I said brightly, in that can-do mummy way women perfect for vaguely uncomfortable situations like nearly losing your toddler at a cafe. The subtext is: 'On a good day I am an excellent mummy, but today I am so tired and fed-up that I am just hoping you can see the funny side.'

'I was like that,' he continued, taking my bank card and punching in my purchase. 'I'm ashamed to say my mum used one of those dog-lead things, after my parents took me to the beach for the day and I kept getting away. The waves were huge and I got wet.'

'Yeah, I had one of those,' I said. It had been an actual dog lead, brown leather, attached to a little white harness, but I didn't mention that. 'Cheaper than the patented child safety lead and just as effective', my mother had told me with pride.

'That's not a good sign!' said my friend, surmising that the toddler-runaway gene is most likely passed through the mother's side.

'Did it work?' I asked the server hopefully. 'Did the dog-lead thing work?'

'It did,' he said, looking down at Micah, by then bored and trying to push his way behind the counter to grab at receipts, 'but I was hyper like that till I was twenty.'

My friend laughed, a little too robustly for my taste, but then she's already raised two busy boys and any humour she can derive from that is well deserved.

'So much to look forward to,' I said, in my false happy voice, transferring Micah onto my hip and heading for the door contemplating the next eighteen years.

Further reading

'Cat-flap Kid's Amazing Adventure' by Michelle Sutton, *Sunday-Star Times*, 1 August 2010

'The Growing Backlash Against Overparenting' by Nancy Gibbs, *Time*, 20 November 2009

'Lights, Camera, Contraction!' by Malia Wollan, *New York Times*, 10 June 2009

'Growing Up in New Zealand: Before We Are Born', Dr Susan Morton et al, University of Auckland, 2010

The Centre for Longitudinal Research, University of Auckland at growingup.co.nz

4. Um, I changed my mind—
I'll get a pony instead
The first weeks at home with baby

Looking back at photos of Micah in his first few weeks of life, I don't even recognise him. He looks like a hairless monkey, wearing a hat and socks. A tiny, mewling, hat-wearing hairless monkey who tipped our little house on its side. My first words when he was handed to me were, 'Oh, he's so *cute*,' and I meant every bit of it. I had worried that I wouldn't be instantly smitten but I need not have spent a nanosecond on that crazy notion: the moment he arrived, Micah became master of my universe.

Nearly all of these photos of brand-new Micah also feature Scout, who looks baffled and intrigued, dear fluffy face tilted to one side. 'What's this?' he seems to ask. 'Is it for me? What do I do with it? Does it roll? Does it belong in the garden? What does it taste like?'

In essence, I felt much the same way as Scout, although

having read a couple of anxiety-producing mothering books and having hungrily listened to every word the nurses said at hospital, I had a working understanding of what I needed to do for my wriggly new master: feed him, burp him, wrap him up warm, walk him outside, jiggle him, sing to him, dance around the kitchen with him—anything to stop the crying and restore peace in our household. Not that Micah was particularly fussy, but when you've never had to care for someone around the clock before it is a shock, even when you've known for months that this day would come. Baby tears are compelling and powerful.

The first few times you bath your baby, change his nappy, dress him in his teddy bear jim-jams and do all these other tasks you have been gagging for a chance to do, it is fun—like playing with a really cool doll. 'Look! He just yawned. Aw, he's reaching out for you. *So cute*.'

I remember thinking during his first nappy change that I didn't see what all the fuss was about, why nappy-changing had become a sitcom classic gag and a subject of dread for new parents. On an academic level it was interesting to see the black tar (meconium) that poured out of him—I was even pleased with myself as I caught the next oozy 'delivery' in a blue cloth as the nurse encouraged me with an enthusiastic, 'Go Mum!'. But by about the tenth nappy change I understood that this repetitive, messy job was going to absorb a lot of my time and that cleaning up after small people is every bit as dull as cleaning up after yourself. Ho hum. Nearly two years later I am still Micah's go-to nappy-changer—he now walks up to me with a nappy in hand saying, 'Bum-bum!' so there is no room for doubt.

I live in central Auckland, which means that after Micah's birth I was entitled to stay at the maternity hospital Birthcare for three nights, a little cushion of me-and-Micah time to usher in this new era. As I lay in bed, a small wooden cot squeezed in beside me, I used the time to get a handle on breastfeeding, attend a workshop on the pelvic floor, and recover a little before heading back to Baby Base Camp. I think we are incredibly lucky to have this service available to us, as any mother who has found herself parked in a wheelchair beside the doors of her local hospital, waiting for a ride home just hours after giving birth, will tell you.

But eventually all new mothers, even spoiled Aucklanders, must face up to their new role. I couldn't wait to get home, to be in my own space, to introduce Micah to his room and his Richard Scarry poster of manic vehicular activity in Busy Town, and his teeny hand-me-down Converse sneakers. I was also, on a more intimate note, tired of people watching me breastfeed. Sometimes I would have three figures gathered round as Micah latched on. Breastfeeding was never a problem for me, for which I am grateful, so all the attention focused on my chest felt a little intrusive.

Still, it was with trepidation that we packed our baby into the back of the newly acquired family wagon and headed back to the hood. (Bought just two months before Micah's arrival, the car had already been broken into when I was picking up his car seat. Who would steal from a heavily pregnant woman?) At first people brought things—lasagne and casserole, flowers and second-hand baby clobber, scented bubble bath and moisturisers. It was wonderful. We received visitors on the deck and entertained them with dodgy anecdotes about oozing black poo and the quality of the view over the city and harbour from the window of our birthing suite. It felt like the Christmas holidays. A lot of wine was drunk. None of it by myself.

We paraded our baby in a series of cosy co-ordinated ensembles, tucked him into his cot, moved him into his capsule, onto a plushy blanket on the floor, into a patch of sunlight, into the pram and off for a walk. We were trying things out, getting acquainted with our options.

We gave Micah his first bath at home, a big production which involved bringing a full-to-the-brim plastic baby bath, several towels, baby powder, rash cream, fresh jammies, extra-sensitive soap and camera into the lounge—our warmest room. We even turned on the underfloor heating in anticipation of this momentous event, which required us to pull the sofa out from the wall and play with a bundle of wires. Tim wrapped Micah in a blanket and cradled him to his chest, while I fiddled with wires and found the right switch. Immediately the lounge filled with the scent of hot dust and wet wool as the floor warmed noticeably in a small patch beneath the coffee table and under a scatter rug.

The moment had arrived. We had the frightening pleasure of dipping our wriggly, bobble-headed baby into water and applying slick-making soap—the whole operation seemed daring and even foolhardy. Scout was intrigued by the bath and kept dodging past us to take a drink of the warm, soapy water. We shooed him away, but he came back for more. It was mayhem.

For a week we inhabited a grey zone, a beginning that felt like it hadn't quite begun. So, we were parents now. Wonderful. We were responsible for this little monkey boy. Fantastic. But there were many unanswered questions. What shape would the days take? How much help would we need from others? When would we start to feel that we were in command of the situation?

We got on with parenting because, at this point, we had no choice. Happily, we were continually amazed by our ability to meet Micah's needs and, more than that, to make him happy, too. It felt good. And then Tim went back to work. The stream of visitors slowed to a trickle, family stepped back a bit to give us space to form our own little family, and I was at a loss as to what to do with myself. There was no structure to this new kind of day. I was too tired and disoriented to do much, and yet I felt like I should be doing much more than I was. It was disconcerting.

I had time now to take stock of myself and I wasn't well pleased with what I found. Giving birth is tough on the female body. Yes, we are designed to do it, although I would argue a button-flap arrangement over the abdomen would make a lot more sense than the traditional birth route. Perhaps with time we will evolve that way. But when your female friends who have been there tell you it feels like you've been hit by a truck, they are only exaggerating a little bit.

You will be tired from your ankle to your eyebrow. As soon as your milk comes in you will find yourself with a pair of chest volleyballs to rival anything you'd pay thousands for in Hollywood. At the same time, your stomach will be deflating in the manner of a forgotten birthday party balloon, a process that can take months, the net effect being that you will look like an out-of-shape Playboy bunny. You have to laugh.

Producing milk is a strange experience, especially if you are not accustomed to farm life, and you may find yourself delivering this life-giving stuff at times when your baby doesn't need it—for example, when you are choosing between the Turkish platter and the calamari salad at your favourite cafe, or scrutinising the closet space at an open home and mentally comparing it to the other house with the weird conservatory that you looked at last weekend, or driving to the gym to do some abdominal exercises that will feel completely pointless and leave you so knackered you actually don't care that your left breast is leaking.

I used to lie on the sofa and wonder what had happened to my life. Was this what I really wanted? What if I had grabbed some of the opportunities I had let slip past me in my twenties? Would I still be here, gently dripping like a faulty tap, if I had done that summer in Florence? If I had gone to a fancier university? If I had kept playing the clarinet and got really, really good instead of really, really loud? If I had got a newspaper job in London during my OE, instead of wasting my days spraying department-store customers with cologne they wouldn't buy?

The answer to all these questions is 'probably not'. I wouldn't have found myself sitting next to Tim at the *New Zealand Herald*, we wouldn't have married, we wouldn't have ended up in the little house in the hood, and we wouldn't have Micah, who is the coolest person I have ever met. Reliving past forks in the road does no-one any good. Still, there is something in the alchemy of those first weeks at home with a baby, when your hormones are surging and ebbing, you are more sleep deprived than ever before, you have time on your hands, and you are adjusting to the overwhelming responsibility of parenthood, that leads you to second-guess yourself—to wonder if the baby in your arms is what you really want after all.

Instead of hating yourself for these thoughts, indulge them for a minute or two. Understand that they are normal and not evil. Your wonderful baby won't know you are mentally cheating on her by envisioning a high-flying career as an astronaut or professional ballroom dancer. Cry, write appalling rhyming journal entries, go out in the garden and have a productive scream—do what you need to do to get it out of your system and then go and put the kettle on.

Without realising it, I slumped into a depressive funk in those first weeks post-baby. The baby blues that arrive on the third day and are supposed to shuffle off by the end of week two hung around for me, eating up the entire winter. When people were with me, I put on a good brave front. Even when health professionals asked me how I was faring, I lied, or minimised my feelings. I am not sure why, although I do like people to view me as capable and reliable, and crying for no reason and obsessing over the thickness of the bedding in Micah's cot and its potential to smother him in his sleep didn't fit with the image I liked to project.

Although I wasn't clinically depressed, I was sad and bewildered much of the time and, to be brutally honest, I wasn't able to fully enjoy my baby for about the first six months of his life. True, I loved him so much I could feel it in my chest, which tightened at the thought of anything bad happening to him, but I also fantasised about leaving him in his cot and driving around the city by myself. That made me feel like an inadequate person, a bad person. I chastised myself for my lack of enthusiasm when so many other women were unable to have babies—would go through just about anything to have their own Micah—and that made me feel worse. The bad feeling fed into itself, like a Celtic snake.

Then I'd see the little Plunket car parked outside our house and for the next hour I wouldn't have to worry about what I should be doing, which was a blessed relief. I boast to women from other countries that in New Zealand we have nurses who come into our homes to check on us in the first weeks after giving birth, who weigh the baby and tell us we're doing a great job, and write lovely notes about us and our children in a book that we get to keep—and they don't believe me. This kind of service for new mums and their babies is precious and unique. As the sensible Plunket nurse made her way up my garden path I felt that, finally, a proper adult had arrived to check on us and make sure everything was tickety-boo—that I was doing okay, that my baby was doing okay, and to reassure me that we weren't alone living on Planet New Baby.

I extrapolated hopefully from the kind and generous things these nurses wrote in Micah's Plunket book. For example:

* 'Beautiful boy. Alert and vigorous.' I would interpret this to mean Micah was the best looking baby the nurse had seen all month, possibly for several years.

* 'Very interested in surroundings.' He's brilliant, I'd think. Who knows what he's thinking about, it could be Proust.
* 'Happy baby. Eleanor doing a great job.' I was not inadequate and lame, after all. I was doing a great job! I was the kind of mum I wanted to be, at least for an hour or so every couple of weeks, when these special women visited my house to see it.

Jane, mother of two, remembers writing in her child's Plunket book: 'Before I had a baby I felt only half alive. Now I have a baby, I feel half dead.' She also told me:

I also remember doing an awful lot of crying. My husband would leave for work with me sitting on the bed, crying and holding a fussy baby who was crying. He came home to much the same picture.

Like many women, Rebecca, mother-of-two, experienced mild depression following the birth of her first son. Because there was so much else going on, she didn't realise it until later, when she was able to look back on those first weeks at home and digest the experience. Here is what she said:

At first I felt like my emotions were all over the place. The tiredness made me feel teary and a bit depressed. After being used to achieving goals and targets at work (and being paid and being able to pay half the mortgage—and buy clothes that don't need to open down the front) I felt like I was getting nothing done apart from sitting on the couch and feeding, changing nappies, washing, and trying to cook something for dinner.

I think I was overwhelmed for a while. I had a long, difficult labour, followed by c-section and feel like I started off on the back foot. The birth wasn't a positive experience and I felt really disappointed about having a c-section for a long time. I had no idea I would feel like this. There is also a bit of an attitude among some women that if you end up having a c-section you have somehow wimped out. Second time around I had luckily got over that and had a scheduled c-section as I felt it was the best option for me and my family. It was!

It requires a radical mind-shift, this baby-arrival business. Returning home after you've had a baby is similar to returning home after your honeymoon—it's a letdown. You've got through the nerve-wracking part of the process (the birth), you've had your amazing in-love, happy happy happy holiday (the first couple of days with baby) and then reality sets in. This is your life now, the die is cast.

Melissa, mother of two, describes her experience:

No-one tells you that the first twelve weeks are both the best and most wonderful weeks of your life as well as the most hideous. The learning curve is extreme, and while I had family support for the first couple of weeks, by week six I was feeling isolated and alone. As I had worked up until twelve hours before going into labour, I had not had a chance to wind down and make that switch from full-on work through to being a mum. That was probably the hardest thing, actually—going from being a professional in a corporate environment where I did a great job, was well respected and seen as an expert in my field, through to fumbling around trying to burp my baby before he got terribly upset. The other major shift was the feeling of not achieving anything—that if I had a shower and made dinner I did well. As I have a strong bias towards achievement, that was difficult for me.

When asked about her first weeks at home with twin boys, Sarah remembers tears:

I was desperately lonely. Desperately in love. Busy, busy, busy. Torturing myself, mentally and physically, over breastfeeding. Exhaustion. Elation. Thinking, 'How long until they're five?'

Mother-of-two Caroline says she muddled through those first days after the birth of her daughter waiting to feel like a real mother:

I was hoping my mothering instinct would rush on in. I had a lot of early trouble with c-section infections, so spent a bit of the first few weeks in hospital feeling tearful and lonely and incapable. With my second, it was a matter of keeping him safe from his sister. The

first few weeks for me were pretty much day to day,
hour to hour. Breastfeeding was painful and dreaded
and considering that's about it for the first four weeks,
I guess I must have been in boob hell!

From the ridiculous to the sublime, those first weeks with
a new baby are like shooting off into a distant galaxy with
Doctor Who when you thought you were just popping down
to the dairy for a litre of milk. Even the most calm and capable
among us will struggle, and some find themselves in a darker
place than they ever imagined possible.

A mother of two on the Oh Baby! mothering forum voiced
the feelings we are never supposed to acknowledge:

I finally understand how people can shake babies out
of tiredness, despair and anger. I lie about understanding that feeling because I don't want to sound like a
psycho.

Joanna spent her first weeks at home with her baby son
greeting a stream of visitors and family, worrying whether
or not she was doing everything 'right'—that's a feeling any
mother will be able to relate to:

I was stressed if the baby didn't sleep or cried when
other people were around. I thought I was a pretty
relaxed, cruisy mum and only realised after I had my
second baby that I wasn't so zen after all.

Gillian, a mother of three, also worried about whether she was doing a good job as a new mum or not, and judged herself harshly for perceived inadequacies:

This may seem strange, but the thing that got me through the first weeks was my husband's cousin who was training to be a paediatrician. She told me it takes a lot to kill a baby. I know this is an odd thing to take comfort from but it made me realise that mistakes could be worked past and not to be too hard on myself.

At the end of the day I just thought, 'I want a happy and healthy baby and so what if I don't get dressed before lunch and we have to have takeaways for dinner again'.

It was a hard-won realisation and one Gillian hesitates to share with others in case they misunderstand her. Even when asked specifically about how she survived early motherhood for this book she apologised for her 'tirade' and said I should feel free to ignore her comments.

Kaila, mother of three, was also frank:

How did I deal with early motherhood? Prayer and antidepressants. No kidding.

By the time you have been at home with your baby for a couple of weeks you'll start getting grilled about what kind of routine you have. I am not sure what the fascination is, and suspect it is simply one of those stock questions considered appropriate to ask new mothers. Well, it's certainly safer than asking, 'Regret it now, don't you?', or 'Is it just me or does he look like a fatter Gollum?'

I didn't have a routine for the first year of Micah's life. I just did whatever seemed like the right thing at the time, an approach that never failed to surprise extended family and seasoned mummy friends. This is a legitimate mothering style, I call it 'attachment parenting meets overwhelmed-mother' syndrome, but it's probably not the best choice for someone who craves order and reason. And actually, babies like the security of knowing that a feed is reliably followed by a play and then a sleep. But in those early months I imagined myself to be standing on a surfboard resting on a thick layer of raspberry jelly spread over an earthquake-prone plain. I'm not sure why, but that's the image that stuck.

When the rumblings started I had to react quickly and skilfully to stay upright. I was Reaction Woman:

* You want to play? Okay, I'll get out the rattles and cloth books and jungle-themed play gym!
* You're hungry? I'll feed you!
* You're sleepy? Okay, I'll snuggle you down in your blanket!
* Not tired, just bored? Let's play peekaboo!
* You're fussy. Let's go outside! We'll look at the birds! We'll sit in the sunshine! We'll go for a walk!

By the time Tim got home from work I often hadn't showered, or brushed my hair, or even changed out of my fluffy pink robe. I had given up on trying to do nice things for myself or my husband, so absorbed was I in caring for the baby. This laser-focus on the new arrival is not necessarily a bad thing, although it is tough on your relationship with your partner, and not always great for your own sense of self. As for me, I felt I had disappeared. There was no time for me as an independent person, separate from this tiny guy with his echoing, gaping abyss of need. Who was I if my baby wasn't near me, defining my days and my function? When my oldest sister-in-law arrived in her loving, bossy way to take Micah for a walk around the neighbourhood so I could sleep, I was grateful but I also felt bereft. When Micah was gone, so was my identity.

Shan, mother of two girls, agrees:

For a while, I don't think I had a view of myself at all. That disappeared in a haze of nappies, vomit and days of running on empty. It was all about just getting through the days. Gradually, I got myself back. My youngest is five now, and I feel like I'm finally ready to be a productive person again—to get some semblance of a life outside mothering back again. I don't regret spending these years as a full-time mum, and am nostalgic about some things, but I am glad to have those baby years behind me.

Writing on the Australian blog mamamia.com, novelist and mother of two children Kylie Ladd said:

I suspect this loss of identity is felt most strongly by those of us who have delayed motherhood to our thirties and forties, who have travelled, become financially independent, enjoyed a good education and rewarding careers, who have bought into the idea that we can have it all.

As a new mum in my mid-thirties I missed my old identity at the same time that I was thrilled by my new one. And terribly frightened by the idea that when my little monkey went to school I would be alone at home, pondering the career that might have been—a premature concern for sure, but there it was, rolling around in my head at 3 am when I was feeding Micah and watching infomercials for collapsible exercise equipment and miniature blenders.

Eventually, as Micah's first birthday approached, Tim and I began to impose some order. We stopped responding immediately to Micah's every squeak. We took the occasional night off and went to the movies, or out to dinner. I stopped breastfeeding just before Micah's birthday. For me, it was a relief and not the sad transition some women experience. Around this time I started to think about returning to part-time work. Gradually, a semblance of my old life returned. Obviously, things will never be the same again, and if I had wanted that, having a child was not the way to go. But it's important to remember that, despite becoming a parent, you have every right to a life of your own. Of course your baby comes first, but that doesn't mean you have to come last after every single member of your family, your neighbours, the grumpy teller at the bank and the slightly gormless girl who sells you fresh bread every Sunday. Don't forget to take time for yourself, and occasionally give yourself top priority.

At the same time, don't forget about your partner. While you are testing the limits to your breastfeeding endurance and losing your rag over neighbours whose revving vehicles wake your baby during nap time, he is expected to get on with everyday life. Sure, he may collect a few congratulatory texts when the baby is born. He may even get taken out for a beer or be presented with a chocolate cigar, ha ha!, but that is usually the extent of it. My sisters-in-law threw me the traditional baby shower with games and blue-iced cupcakes and lots of presents. Tim was not invited. But one kind friend who had been shoved to the perimeter three times when his wife had a baby gave Tim a wrist rattle for Micah, which was a lovely gesture that still makes me smile.

For the most part, mums get all the credit for having produced this new little person. They get the parties, the flowers of congratulations and the extra-special 'Well dones' after the birth. But no woman ever becomes a mother without assistance and we shouldn't forget that the lives of new fathers—or, if the father's not on the scene, your support crew—are also upended and reformed. As much as life with a newborn can feel like a solo battle while you're in the trenches day after day and your partner is safely going about their business as usual, his life has also irrevocably changed.

Many relationships come under intense pressure and begin to splinter when babies arrive. While I realise you already have more than enough on your plate, make an effort to stay connected to your partner or support people. You need them to be healthy and happy so they can help keep you healthy and happy. And don't forget, they have been waiting for this baby to arrive just as long as you have.

Bear in mind that your partner, too, will be tired and bewildered. He may be feeling burdened with his increased financial responsibility. As Tim says:

Your expectations of manhood and personal success are changed with fatherhood. Guys are also thrown into suddenly having to be this thing you've never been before—a father. They also have to balance the joy and gain of new parenthood with the guilty grief for what's lost.

When Tim and I moved to my California birthplace for a late OE prior to having a family, we worked for a time at a mega-bookstore. It was massive, with its own in-house Starbucks, a music store, many expansive sofas, and a loyalty programme we were expected to promote like nerdy heroin pushers. For the first couple of weeks it was fun—the discount was great, the over-educated staff were fascinating, the coffee was good. Tim became frighteningly adept at selling loyalty cards, gracing the top of the staff noticeboard and earning the suspicion of the perpetually disgruntled woman who usually held the number one spot. But once we had mastered the cash registers and the online catalogue it rapidly got boring and we started looking for better jobs.

We developed an iron-clad policy: no spouse left behind,

our version of George Bush's 'no child left behind' educational plank. As soon as one of us got a different job, we were both outta there. And so it came to pass. When I was hired to be associate editor of a university-based magazine, Tim resigned too, embarking on an enviable freelance career that involved going to the local Cuban cafe for spiced hot chocolate and blogging for the *Guardian*, and later a full-time job editing travel stories for a bunch of web entrepreneurs who, predictably, called him 'Kiwi'.

New parenthood felt much the same. It wouldn't be fair for Tim to maintain the social life and work schedule he had before Micah arrived. He had to make allowances for the fact that I was marooned at home with a baby who relied on me for every meal, who cried if I so much as went to the loo without him. But it was equally important for me not to hog all the baby responsibility, or to micromanage Tim's interaction with his son. We tried to approach new parenthood in solidarity: no spouse left behind. It didn't always work, and two years on there are still occasions when I am annoyingly bossy about Micah's nap times or Tim forgets that I can never, *never*, simply pick up my bag and walk out the door. That I have to plan every activity as if it were a minor military op: Operation Mother Freedom. At least we're aware of these issues, and that is 90 per cent of the battle won.

Mothers interviewed for this book told me they reclaimed their romantic relationships with their partners after the newborn phase was completed, and parenthood often made their bond stronger and better. As Jackie, mother of two, says:

Babies and little people can take up so much of your time that in many ways your relationship with your partner goes pretty much out the window for a while, especially in the early days when Mum is so indispensable, particularly if she's breastfeeding.

In the face of that intense baby–mother relationship, it is important that a mother considers her partner's needs too. While sex is going to be at the bottom of your to-do list for some months—and may even hurt for a while after giving birth—it is critical to maintain some time for you and your partner, away from baby and baby's needs. Don't let new parenthood drive a wedge between you, as it does for so many couples.

Here is the voice of experience from Jo, mother of one, who has had thirteen years to develop a parenting strategy with her husband:

We are a solid team, we tag team when things get really tough and we agree rules in advance.

Mother-of-three Gillian and her husband take a similar approach:

It's us against them. We were married for ten years before we had children and he is still the first person I choose to spend time with. It just felt like a natural extension of our relationship, sort of like adding an exciting new room but the rest of the house is still there and strong.

It's not easy though, as Joanna, mother of two, says:

Kids soak up a lot of your emotions and there's less left for your partner. I'm more impatient with him, less tolerant. It's a broad sweep, but I put them first, he puts himself first and our relationship can fall through the gap. And it's just busy, being working parents.

After a month or so, when you are feeling more on top of this whole baby lark, you will be ready to leave the house. It is quite the task. You shouldn't attempt it too soon for fear of putting yourself off attempting it again any time in the next six months or so. People used to tell me that despite appearances an infant was the easiest kind of child to take out because they were constantly falling asleep, leaving you free to catch up with your friends, find Christmas presents, and get your GP check-up. 'This is the time to go to cafes and restaurants,' my dear friend, a mother-of-two, advised sagely. 'Once they can *move*, it is so much harder.'

Now that I have a toddler, her words really resonate because my curious young man won't be quiet and still for anything . . . *any blessed thing*. I choose to meet friends at cafes with playhouses and spaces where he can run free or, if I am feeling less robust, at a playground or our own child-oriented home. I distract him with fluffies which he pours down his legs, and tidbits from my meal which he may chew for a while before pulling them out of his mouth and handing them to me politely with a 'Ta' or 'Done'. He will play with his cars for a short time, sharing his bonhomie with the whole cafe. 'BOOM' he might say as one car collides with another. As charming as this sounds, other patrons are not always delighted by my boy. Taking him out is a delicate balance between meeting my needs and his, but also between my respect for people sharing public spaces with us and my belief that children deserve respect, too.

Just getting out the door is a feat and a half. First you have to gather a boatload of stuff—spare clothes, hats, bibs, toys, books, changing gear, snacks—and wedge it all into the nappy bag, if you can bear it. These days, when I'm feeling on top of things, I will often just stow a spare nappy and some wipes in my handbag next to my wallet and chewing gum and head off feeling giddy and reckless and carefree. But back at the beginning I was devoted to my heavy sack of baby paraphernalia and I usually needed all of its contents. Once you have packed the bag, you need to make sure the baby is clean and dressed before venturing out for fear someone will decide to pick on you while you browse the aisles at Countdown.

I have also found that it helps to have a well-presented baby when some well-meaning but confrontational older woman asks why you think it is necessary to leave the house with a newborn when, in her day, it was three months before new mothers ever went anywhere. It is also good if you have taken the time to brush your hair, so the well-meaning but confrontational older woman doesn't feel the need to also tsk-tsk you for being unkempt.

There will be repeated attempts to gain momentum as

your child fills his nappy and spits up on himself. By this time 45 minutes will have passed, he will be hungry and you will need to stop and feed him. You may also be hungry, too, and require a quick pick-me-up. Then your beloved will phone from work to check on his firstborn and you will rehash your morning: laundry, nap time, feeding, playtime, feeding, walk around the block. Finally, two hours after you first thought it might be nice to pick up some hummus and a copy of the new *Grazia*, you will make it out the door.

Despite the giant bag, many times in those early months when I was out with Micah trying to reconnect with life beyond my street I would find myself lacking some essential item, such as a fresh nappy, those magical scented bags for storing used nappies when you're on the run, or a spare dummy. It was so dispiriting, because I knew my shot at meaningful interaction with the world was gone for that day. Once I made it home to the nappy and dummy supply centre I would be too tired to venture out again. I would sink into the comforts contained within my own four walls and my baby would be delighted to be reunited with his play mat and soft blocks.

But first I had to get back to the hood, and that was no simple task. When a baby wants something, they want it *now*. They will not be reassured by your repeated insistence that 'It's okay, darling, we're going home now.' In a baby's mind 'If I don't have it now, I may never get it. Shit!' Many times, with a squalling Micah in tow, I would trot back to the car, wrestle him into his car seat, and turn on some music I knew he liked, usually Simon and Garfunkel or Springsteen. Still he would howl, and I would feel my shoulders creeping towards my ears and all my muscles tensing as I drove home with a screaming ball of pure hot willpower, hitting every red light as luck and the universe would have it. Ah, yes. Precious memories.

It is only fair that I warn you now: with a new baby in the house your social life is officially stalled. You are going nowhere fun tonight . . . or tomorrow night . . . or any other night for the next four months or so. Our first night out together sans baby came when Micah was five months old and able to go more than two hours without a feed. We planned an evening at the ballet: a single glass of chardonnay for me (which felt illicit and inappropriate and quite, quite wonderful), a beer for Tim, some adult company, pretty costumes, a few grands jetés, and then back home to baby.

We left the house at 7.15 pm for a 7.30 pm performance. Now, if I still lived in Gisborne this would be fine. Normal. But living in central Auckland means this is a choice only a fool or adrenaline junkie would make. At 7.16 pm Tim, a man who never arrives anywhere on time and takes it as a point of pride that he's never the one doing the waiting, received a text from our niece who was also attending the ballet. 'We're here, whereabouts are u?'

A minute later I received the same text. 'Gosh, they're vigilant,' said Tim, who had already amassed seven nieces and nephews before we met, plus a few godchildren. He likes to run his fingers up his neck à la Don Corleone and call himself The Godfather.

'Oh, they're just bored cos they arrived at the ballet half an hour early,' I said, smugly.

As we sailed down Kepa Rd I remembered that the Aotea Centre locks latecomers out of performances. That you have to wait for the interval. I could just imagine how this would strike Tim—40 minutes on a rectangular black sofa reading the programme, intolerable!—so concocted a back-up plan to save our precious evening out. If we were locked out of the first act, we would decamp to Borders for a browse. I could point out the lavender filofax I had recently admired (before I saw the $233 price tag and had a very loud negative reaction to the news). We would peruse the bargain tables. It would be fine.

Stopped at the lights at Albert Street I was almost sure we would be locked out of the first act and I felt sad about this. I had been daydreaming about a night out for months.

Undaunted, hubby gunned it down the slope into the Civic car park. Staff in yellow vests stepped out from their little cubicle in a 'maayte, what's your story?' sort of way but we kept wheeling round the car park like boy racers. Later, we found on our windshield a cross note from the yellow vests alerting us to the car park's ten kph speed limit and warning us that next time we tried to park there our car might be towed.

We snorted, which is not the sort of behaviour responsible adults in possession of a small person engage in, and yet it was pretty funny. Because the yellow vests had to hunt down our car to leave the note, perhaps even replaying surveillance camera footage to see which floor we ended up on. That must have taken some time.

We jumped out of the car and ran up the stairs towards Aotea Square.

'This is exciting!' I said.

'That's the spirit!' said Tim.

He fleet-footed it past the construction barriers. I had to slow down to negotiate wet concrete in pointy boots. I felt winded but could see other latecomers jogging across the foyer. We were the last ones to take our seats. The lights were already dimmed and the dancers were just trit-trotting onto the stage, all glowy and lovely. The efforts of the dancers on stage were intensified by my own recovery-breathing. We were simpatico.

For Tim this was the ideal result—not a moment was wasted in preparation for our night at the ballet. He waited for no-one. I was happy because I was not locked out. Micah was safe at home with Granny and Scout. That evening marked a return to life as we had always known it, not the hazy half-life of recent months in which we communicated almost solely about tasks we had to complete and performed those tasks in robotic fashion, always looking for the first opportunity to sneak off for a sleep. It was a turning point and we celebrated by cackling about yellow-vested car park staff all the way home.

Here are survival tips for taking baby home:

* People genuinely want to help when you have a newborn, especially if they have been there themselves. Never turn down an offer of help.

* Whenever anybody offers you the chance to take a nap while they mind the baby, take it. Even if you do not yet feel like the walking dead, you soon will. Relax while the opportunity is there. Read a book or magazine if you're not sleepy. Reacquaint yourself with what is happening in the world outside your house.

* If someone offers to make you dinner, say, 'Yes, please'.

* If you have a pet who becomes jealous of the new arrival, make sure there is someone around to make a fuss of them. In our case, this was my mother, who stayed with us when Micah was born. She brought Scout squeaky presents, and let him sleep on her bed.

* If you get tired when visitors are around, politely excuse yourself and go and lie down. They won't mind—if they do, for heaven's sake don't invite them back.

* Let your partner do as much baby care as he wants. You have a natural urge to spend as much time with the baby as possible and protect him or her at all times. This is as it should be, but don't forget that the baby's father also wants to bond with the newbie. Let him have his time. Habits formed now will set you in good stead a year or two from now when you want to nip down to the pub to meet your girlfriends.

* Some babies—about twenty per cent—are born irritable. Truly. Psychologist Jerome Kagan proved it years ago.

Bear that in mind if your mother-in-law or bossy neighbour tries to imply that your baby is grizzly because you are not doing your job properly. It might just be that you got a grumpy baby.

* Remember, the first weeks at home with your newborn are a stage—they are a very short period in your life, even though it will feel as if you've been a slave to this child for 100 years. You will not be stuck scrutinising the colour of your lounge walls forever. You will eventually get some energy back. You will, with time, remember who you are.

* If you haven't already done so, invest in MySky. You will spend more time at home than you ever thought possible and you will need some mindless entertainment, because babies sleep a lot and books may require more concentration than you can muster.

Further reading

Thriving Under 5, Plunket, 2009

Well Child Tamariki Ora Health Book, Ministry of Health, 2008

Plunket at plunket.org.nz

Little Treasures at treasures.co.nz

OH baby! at ohbaby.co.nz

5. Coffee group dropout
Making friends with other mothers

By the time Micah was six months old he could roll over, squeal like a dolphin for 40 minutes at a time and blow raspberries. He had sprouted two teeth and a wonderfully silly sense of humour and he liked to play with his feet. In the time he made these great strides towards becoming a more fully functioning person, his mother had bombed out of two coffee groups. It seems I am not the only one. Danielle, survivor of two coffee groups, describes her experience:

> The first group was really competitive and not very nice to each other, always excluding people and backstabbing. I joined another one after a kindergarten mum asked me to join, but the mothers were all more concerned about talking to each other rather than doing things for the kids, and their kids were particularly

funny about not wanting others to join in and weren't that nice to my kids, so we left that one too.

I just couldn't handle the competition, the back-handed compliments and the nastiness. You think you're going to a cosy gathering of like-minded women to eat cupcakes and laugh about those people who throw themselves in front of you when you go to the Warehouse, trying to convince you take your baby to Pixi Photo. But there's a hidden agenda at work, and you just end up feeling bad about yourself and wondering what the heck happened to sisterhood.

The straw that broke this mummy's back was a conversation about bananas. I had hauled myself to my last-ever coffee group meeting after a night of sleeping hi-jinks. Micah had been up five times the night before . . . and the night before that . . . and the night before that. And he had performed the same trick the preceding week. I was so tired that my eyeballs hurt and I couldn't remember really basic stuff, like where I had left the keys. I thought if anyone would understand my situation it would be other new mothers so dragged myself out and along to the group in search of some support.

So, when I turned up at the coffee thing 45 minutes late and explained the sleeping debacle, I paused to let the comforting tide of sympathy wash over me. Nothing. Eventually, the woman seated next to me said, 'And I thought *my baby* was bad.' This is classic coffee group behaviour—the sneaky put-down cloaked in commiseration. You don't realise what has really happened until the moment has passed and it's too late to respond. Instead, you take a fortifying gulp of coffee and put your baby on the play mat in the middle of the room and wait for him to be judged. And let me just say, Micah was not *bad*, folks. He was a little baby doing what little babies do, which is not fitting in with my agenda and not giving a fig that his behaviour is inconvenient to me.

So, on that occasion, not to be bowed, and in a slightly desperate way it must be said, I told a little story about how Micah could roll from his back to his front and his front to his back and how his father had never seen it and was starting to wonder if I was, in fact, making it up, tee hee. I know it's not an anecdote I could use on the *Late Show with David Letterman*, but hey, I was tired and making an effort to be friendly—it *had* to be at least as interesting as the interrogation another mum was being subjected to concerning where she was getting her baby's non-branded nappies. Turned out Micah was not only the sole roller in the group, but he was also the only possessor of teeth. Genius, I know. This seemed to tick off one mum who wanted to know *how* I was *sure* he could roll. 'Um, well, I've seen it,' I said, wondering what sort of evidence she required. At that moment Micah was reaching for a teething ring and happily settled on his back. He did not look like he was going to be rolling any time soon. Ticked-off Mum remained unconvinced, giving him a look that seemed to say, 'You don't look quite bright enough to roll, buddy.' And then came the bananas bit. Because he was the only baby with teeth, I was asked what he was eating. Solids once a day, I said. Apple, pear, blah, blah, boring blah, carrot, pumpkin, kumara, mango, banana . . . And someone piped up with, 'You have to be careful with banana. You can't give a baby a banana like you or I would eat, you have to give them a really ripe one, or they can get sick.'

'Oh, that's okay,' I said blithely, 'I give him banana from a jar. He doesn't eat much, so I haven't started puréeing food for him yet.' (Admission: I never puréed anything for Micah. By the time he had six or eight teeth he was demanding adult food and I was more than happy to give it to him.) She looked deeply unimpressed. 'That just seems like too much work right now,' I explained.

She replied, 'What, it's too hard to mash a banana?' Meeeoow. *I know, right?* I laughed it off by half-pie admitting that, yes, I am so crap I can't even manage to mash a banana. Ha, ha. But I was actually really mad.

What does it matter where a baby's food is coming from as long as it's nutritionally sound? And what business was it of hers whether I made my own baby food or bought endless jars of expensive goop from the supermarket? I mean, who cares? It turns out a surprisingly high number of people do care about this mundane stuff, although to them it is not mundane but incredibly important and indicative of the quality of your credentials for raising a small human. I had been exposed as lacking the fortitude required to raise a child properly. If I couldn't muster the energy or commitment to mash a b-a-n-a-n-a, what else was I failing to do?

In the car, I comforted myself with the knowledge that the people whose opinion mattered to me, like Micah's doctor and the Plunket nurse, always said he was flourishing.

He was happy, healthy, and cute as a button mushroom. One other mother's opinion was irrelevant, but it stung. My standard response to anyone else's baby has always been, 'Oh, isn't he/she beautiful. Just beautiful.' I don't think there is anything else you need to say. Later, Tim provided comfort and the perfect comeback: 'You should have told her you don't purée food because you don't love your baby as much as she loves her baby.'

My reservations about coffee groups are shared by many women I spoke to for this book. Angela, mother of one:

I remember some of my early coffee group meetings where some of the mothers seemed to be coping incredibly well—one of them was baking while her daughter was sleeping during the day—and this was at a stage where I couldn't even feed myself and get dressed without help because I had no time and was completely overwhelmed.

Julie, mother of two, looks back:

Our 'nappy group' met weekly for years. Trouble was they were all wealthy and I felt I wasn't providing enough for my kids—we didn't teach our kids to ski, for example—plus they went to private schools and though they were friendly I felt we did compare kids too much. So maybe they weren't really true friends, but they helped at the time.

Like many social constructs, coffee groups have a use-by date. While you hear tales of warm and loving coffee groups that still get together to celebrate their children's 21st birthdays, they are a rarity. Most women drift away from their coffee groups soon after their babies are weaned, sooner if they return to work. But many women still crave a group of like-minded mother-friends with whom they can share their experiences—women who will understand when they cancel plans at the last minute because a child has a fever, and who understand why it's no longer fun to stay out until 2 am.

Mother-of-two Maree's experience seems to be typical:

I did the coffee group thing for the first eighteen months and in the initial stages I have to say it was very helpful—but that was while the babes were small and just adorable little lumps of cooing, pooey, drooling love. Once they started all those 'milestone' stages, the competitive nature of all these women came out. I checked out pretty quickly after that.

Melissa found she grew apart from her coffee group friends after returning to full-time work:

My coffee group was a life raft when we first got together when my son was about six weeks old. We have all grown apart now that half of us are back working, so I only keep in contact with one person from that group. To be honest, most of my friends are not 'mummy friends', even those that have children. We tend to get together and hang out without our children.

Deborah, mother of two, doesn't even like the sound of 'mummy friends' and rejected the coffee group idea outright:

How revolting. I have enjoyed making friends with women who also have children but would never phrase it like that. I do find it easier to be friends with other women who have children—I like seeing the kids playing together while we have a wine and a goss—and some of my friends without kids have rather fallen by the wayside.

Jackie, mother of two boys, says:

I have to admit, I didn't enjoy the whole playgroup/mother's group thing. I don't drink tea and I found it really hard to sit around for hours talking about nothing but babies. I craved the company of other adults. I lived and breathed babies 24/7, the last thing I wanted to do was talk about it some more!

Gillian was living overseas, in a country where English is not the first language, when she had her first child so missed out on the coffee group thing:

It was not until my daughter was past one that I connected with other mothers at a church coffee group.

I found church good as we come from the same faith base and in some ways this negated our vastly different parenting styles and it felt supportive rather than judgmental. I have found it harder to maintain these friendships as school and after-school activities drag me so many different ways. I miss them.

On the other hand, Bonnie, mother of two and an unrepentant coffee-group dropout, remembers:

When I had my first child, I was promised—by the media, the women's mags I read at the dentist's, and some kind of absorbed mothering mythology—that my days at home would be rich with new friendships, forged through the shared bonds of supportive mothers' groups. Instead I discovered the Olympic sport I called 'mother-upship'. The coffee groups were either deathly boring, even to the sleep deprived mind—I mean there's only so much discussion of nappies one can take—or viciously competitive. After a while I realised everyone was lying through their teeth about the achievements, especially nocturnal ones, of their little darlings. But that was it for me. I went back to my job in political lobbying—much more supportive, friendly and way less competitive!

Bonnie also says coffee groups serve as an introduction to the ugly side of competitive mothering, and that things can get much worse as your child grows:

Of course it does not end with babies, especially if you live in Auckland. It's called school and 'parental involvement in the life of the school'. I am a dropout from that as well. It's mother-upship with bells on. Take my advice, make a mental note to stay out of that one before you even get there.

Dita, mother of two, fitted right into the coffee group dynamic:

> . . . because I was always the type of woman to go to coffee groups, join Plunket committees, attend play-groups. I know for some women it's like watching paint dry, but for me I found staying at home much too maddening.

Personally, I thought there would be nothing nicer than finding a group of new friends to drink coffee with and talk about whatever we fancied as our small children grew up together. Coffee group sounded to me like the sort of thing Carol Brady would be part of, and I grew up thinking Carol Brady was just about the keenest mother ever. Many women do find coffee groups incredibly supportive, a real lifeline in a time of shifting sands. But I have heard many, many tales like mine of coffee groups gone wrong, and the embarrassment of dropping out, or the fear of offending another mother—espe-cially if she is a hyper-competitive alpha mother who will never let you forget your transgression.

The problem, comes, I think, when we assume that every

new mother will want to be in a coffee group and that every coffee group is a place of refuge and friendship when that is demonstrably not the case. You see women making pleading attempts to form coffee groups on online forums, some after they have failed to gel with the coffee group that grew from their antenatal class. It's heartbreaking.

Having given it a fair bash, I would never bother with a coffee group again. My book club is a useful stand-in, and if I am really stuck I have a doctor, three sisters-in-law, and a bunch of friends who also happen to have children. I am like Sarah, mother of two, who says:

> I tend to be friends with people because I like them, not because they have children. I have met some lovely women through kindy and school, but very few would be close friends, more support.

It is a cruel twist of new motherhood that at the time when you need friends most you are not in a position to nurture friendships. A lot of people will understand—will overwhelm you with their love and support—but others will, sadly, drop out of your life. This might be because they haven't had children and do not realise the all-consuming nature of babies, or because they desperately want children and watching you cuddling your baby stabs them in the heart or, possibly, they just aren't interested in your new status. None of these situations is insurmountable, but it may take time for both sides to adjust.

While I still hope for a fun crop of new mummy friends,

and have heard kindergarten can be a useful source—joining committees is the key, apparently—I am content, for now, to maintain longstanding friendships that have taken a hit in these baby years, just like everything else. Jane, mother of two, explains:

> Friends weren't a biggie when the kids were young—I was too busy parenting and working and maintaining a friendship with my husband. Just no time for me and my needs! We had no extended family help available until the kids got to school, so simply no time for extras. Friends are an extra, over and above parenthood.

Gillian, mother of three, says:

> The friends I made from kindergarten and school are different types, more superficial. I have drifted away from some people and towards others who share my parenting approach. I can't give further explanation without sounding like a judgmental bitch.

As a new mother you will be thrown into social settings that are quite foreign. Besides the dreaded coffee group, there are baby music classes, baby birthday parties, baby swimming lessons (watch out for the bouncy 'fun mum' in the teeny bikini), and play dates in the park (which are really opportunities for you to try to find some mummy friends who actually share your values, interests and sense of humour). As a new mother you may assume that everyone else has got their groups sorted and that you are the girl who joined the cheering squad two weeks after everyone else and never quite caught up—doomed to catch the ends of conversations and wonder if those girls were talking about you. You'd be surprised how many other women feel left out of the mummy circle.

Writing in *Little Treasures* magazine, Alexia Santamaria, mother of two boys, said:

When I had my first child I experienced a real shift in my friendships. Spontaneous coffees had become precise, planned operations and my tequila all-nighters were now teething all-nighters. I found myself out of the loop as friends without children forgot to invite me to things or assumed I couldn't come. On top of the fact that my life had changed forever, it was all a bit of a downer.

She started searching for mummy friends, at a music group, play group and, finally, the park, where she spied a woman in an eye-catching red winter coat:

I went through the usual agony of wondering if it looked too desperate to ask for her number, but decided to get over myself.

Like Alexia, Maree has struggled to hold on to her childless friends now that she has two young boys:

Many just can't cope with what time-consuming, unpredictable, smelly, messy, noisy little things children can be. Also when you have children you get very good at planning in advance around naps, feeds, babysitters—many childless friends just struggle to get that.

I am even a reluctant music group mum. I do it because my boy loves to make noise, and I love to see him bursting with joy as he wiggles from side to side, Stevie Wonder-style, and also because it tires him out and guarantees at least one decent nap a week. But I am not a natural fit for this brand of organised fun, like many women who find themselves holding a pair of teensy brass cymbals and singing about the wheels on the bus.

When we lived in San Francisco one of my daily pleasures was passing the chi-chi baby music group headquarters a block down the street from our apartment. A large picture window offered a view into a bizarre and exotic world that I found both repellent and magnetic: hip mums and dads in ultra-pricey skate shoes and tight jeans sat cross legged in a circle with tiny, colour-coordinated babies in their laps. The babies slumped there drooling, while the mums and dads shook maracas and beat on little drums and sang awkwardly about rainbows and teddy bears, making exaggerated happy faces and occasionally leaning down, wide-eyed, their mouths in Os of feigned surprise, to show their babies how much fun they were having. The gap between the hipness of the parents and the dorkiness of their attendance at a baby music class was heartwarming.

My sister-in-law leads a church-based music group and she is amazing—enthusiasm personified. She will put on a train conductor's hat and chugga-chug-chug around the room leading a conga line of delighted little people by the hand. She will wear a clownish rainbow wig and mark the beat on an old cake tin. She will open up the 'special box' and feign surprise at the helium balloon she finds inside, or the bird puppet, or the shiny red apple.

I often sit and watch her and Micah and all the other small people and wonder if this is one of those situations in which I can fake it till I make it, or if I am destined to slide through baby music like I slid through sixth-form mathematics—reluctantly and with a snarky attitude. I sing, 'The green means go and red means stop, stop, stop!' but my heart's not in it. The red could just as well mean three-yearly cervical smear, or $400 anti-wrinkle serum, or 10k run, for all the fun I get out of it. But I do love to see Micah clapping his hands after each song crying, 'Mo-ah, mo-ah! Yah!' and turning to me to check that I am clapping, too.

This is when I break out my O of feigned surprise, the one that used to make me smirk when I caught the San Francisco parents using it, and Micah shrieks, stamps his little feet and points excitedly, 'Yah!'. I realise that baby music may be slightly uncomfortable for me, but it is like freaking Disneyland for Micah, and that is the main thing and why I persevere.

Not so easy to negotiate is the free-play time after class, when Micah, hopped-up on vanilla wine biscuits and music endorphins, sometimes loses his grip on appropriate social behaviour. If he is sitting on the plastic crocodile see-saw and another toddler comes over for a turn, he will reach out and swat them like a moth, saying, 'Go away, go away'. If someone else wants to play with the cars and garage set, with those superb ramps and petrol pumps, he will knock them off their feet. The other child's tears of dashed hope have no effect on him. He is a piece of granite until I haul him off to the room where all the prams are parked to think about his actions, and then he is a river of molten lava.

'Go away, Mummy!' he will scream, scissoring his legs and howling for his lost toy.

'Micah, no hitting. We don't hit,' I will explain sharply, as he wriggles to get free. 'Micah, look at me. No hitting. You have been a naughty boy.'

'No naughty! Good boy,' Micah will say. 'Gooood boy.'

These situations are always worse if the other child's mother has seen my bruiser strike their baby. I always worry that my response seems weak and ineffectual, that they are secretly judging my special little man on the basis of an isolated, albeit disturbing, incident without knowing all the wonderful things about him: that he kisses his cousins without being asked, that he loves to watch pukekos in the swamp behind our house, that every time he stubs a toe or scrapes an elbow he asks for 'oint', that he thinks his daddy can fix anything, from a broken rocking horse to a faulty radio.

I am a more enthusiastic participant in the tried and trusted trip to the park, probably because there are more elements that I can control, although sometimes unexpected circumstances arise, like when the other mother brings snacks enough for everyone while all you have are a couple of wine biscuits and a handful of cereal which you dole out to the other children—better fed children who are accustomed to packets of real-fruit jelly babies and organic English-cheddar flavoured crackers and look at you like, 'Really? Is that the best you can do?' Shame. The only real warning I would offer for the park play-date is that sometimes bigger kids will use the equipment intended for toddlers and this will enrage you more than you could expect—*because they have their own danged playground*! Because they are *big*! Because they don't give a fig what you have to say to them! And because you don't dare say what you really think because it is unclear which sunbathing mum within earshot is theirs.

Birthday parties are an interesting microcosm of your social set. For example: there's the homemade train cake versus the professionally baked zoo cake; games in the back garden versus activities at a for-hire party venue; a piece of cake in plastic wrap to take home versus a goody bag stuffed with stickers and colouring sets and plastic tops and lollies and balloons and rubber balls and stamps and tickets to *Disney on Ice*. There's also the family-only party, which is as much about Nana and Poppa as it is about the birthday child, versus the friends and neighbours party which is really about keeping people sweet. When throwing birthday parties, we reveal a lot about our parenting philosophies, and guests will take note, don't you worry. But your child? He will focus on the wrapping paper and ribbons, the cake and any opportunities to ride trikes, climb things or make a mess.

Now that Micah attends a childcare centre, I have a new

crop of mummy events to attend. The first of these was an afternoon tea at which we received little white canvases embellished with our children's handprints in paint—blue for the boys and pink for the girls. We were fed chocolate and scones with cream and jam and did a preschool education-themed quiz that was so complicated I don't think a winner was ever found. It was fun, and without exception each mother I spoke to said, 'I wasn't going to come to this.' There is a widespread fear out there that mummy events are just another opportunity to have your nose rubbed in your inadequacies. That the vast majority of mothers are mean girls dressed up as somebody's mum. It is sad.

The Christmas party was a bigger gathering—dads came too. We had to take a snack for morning tea. When I handed over my chocolate cake, bought from Countdown and prettied up with some past-their-use-by-date silver dragées from the pantry, I felt lacking. Homemade was definitely the order of the day. The table groaned under the weight of thick slabs of caramel slice and fudge, tiny cupcakes covered in buttercream icing and sprinkles, shortbread in whimsical shapes, and there was the obligatory (untouched) platter of vegetable sticks. Then I thought, 'Sod it' and joined Micah in the playground, where he was dancing to the beat of his own imagined music.

Further reading

'Come here often?' by Alexia Santamaria, *Little Treasures*,
October/November 2010

Daphne Brogdon at coolmom.com

Mindy Roberts at themommyblog.net

6. I don't care about world peace, or environmental disaster, or who wins *MasterChef*, I just want a decent night's sleep

Lack of sleep makes you crazy. This is not an idle threat. It really does, and we are talking about the kind of tired that you feel in your bones and in your hair follicles. It makes your eyeballs hurt and lends your skin a nasty greyish tint. It makes you believe everyone, including your beloved bundle, is out to get you.

For many months following the birth of my son I was actually nervous about leaving the house for fear of behaving inappropriately due to exhaustion caused, mainly, by lack of sleep. I was tearful and paranoid and angry a lot of the time. After a day spent minding the boy—anxious that I would do something wrong because I had never been around tiny babies before, and I was so very heartbreakingly, achingly tired—I often regarded any further demands on my time and energy to be hostile.

'You want me to pay bills *now*? I am on my way to bed!' I would shrill at my husband in a fairly typical exchange.

'I could use your help,' he'd say, perfectly reasonably, for I too had used power and water that month, and it was usually me who had left the unopened bills sitting on the dining table to gather dust.

'Seriously, *now*?' This was accompanied by the universal gesture of martyrdom, also known as the 'you wanna piece of this, chump?' gesture, seen in all movies set in New Jersey—arms held out to the sides, hands open, palms exposed. Go ahead, make my day, sucker. Realising his wife was about to blow her top in spectacular fashion, possibly waking the baby and further deteriorating the situation, Tim would say, 'Never mind. Go to bed.'

'I just need some sleep!'

'I know you do, sweetheart.'

Melissa, mother of two, feels the same way:

The only time now that I have deep sleep and don't wake up is if I get a nap when the kids aren't here or if I am travelling for work and sleeping in a motel room. I am constantly aware on some level that I am responsible for my kids during the night, and given my propensity for worrying anyway, I am the type of person who will wake at 2 am and have to go and check 'just in case'.

At seventeen months, Micah still didn't reliably sleep through the night. On the odd occasion he did, it was because he had first spent two hours subverting the bedtime routine, wearing himself out in the process. Toying with us by drinking his bottle—usually the precursor to sleepy snuggles and cot time—and climbing down off his preferred parent-of-the-day's lap to dig around in his plastic toy buckets, saying, 'Car, car, car? Book?', he managed to postpone the inevitable. When your kid gets to this age, they possess surprising strength and willpower. The bedtime battle can turn into a physical one, with a kicking, twisting, screaming toddler making it absolutely clear that they won't go anywhere quietly. In our house we would often just get Micah settled and then realise we were too tired ourselves to do anything but follow his snuffling example.

When Micah was about six months old and I could no longer stand the constant inquiries as to his sleep-time habits by virtually every person I ever saw, from family and friends to the woman behind the counter at PaperPlus, I went to a seminar on how to get your baby to sleep through the night. I was late, of course. I don't think I have ever arrived anywhere on time since I had Micah—he is a time-suckage machine. Anyway, as I made my way towards an empty seat, I noticed that all the other mothers had brought their partners with them. Mine was at home looking after Micah, but I was mad at him all the same. Why couldn't he support me at this seminar, the selfish monkfish? See—*crazy*.

There followed an hour in which a woman with five thousand children, groovy jewellery and enviably springy hair told us something we all knew in our hearts but didn't want to act on: your child will sleep if you put him in his cot and leave him, even if he cries, kicks his feet and (in the case of my wilful toddler) shouts, 'Up, up, up, up!' Eventually, he will give up and go to sleep. *Because he has no choice.* Around the room heads bobbed up and down, pens scribbled on notepads, and there was a sense of relief. Anyone who had left their child to cry was vindicated and everyone else was given the all-clear to try it. Here comes the 'but', because neither I nor the sleep-seminar woman advocate the so called 'cry it out' method for babies under nine months of age: it is stressful for them, and you. Your baby will feel safe and cared for if you respond to their needs quickly and calmly around the clock in the first months of life. That's just part of your job.

Some experts, Dr Miriam Stoppard prime among them, believe a baby under twelve months should never be left to cry without reassurance from a caregiver because it hinders their emotional and intellectual development. High levels of the stress hormone cortisol, which babies produce in large quantities during episodes of unanswered crying, are damaging for a baby's developing brain. Babies do not have a mechanism for dealing with stress. Babies are designed so that their stress is managed by a parent, who responds to crying with reassuring cuddles and who tries to meet their needs as quickly and efficiently as possible. When this doesn't happen they become more wound up, more vulnerable to stress, and feel less secure than is good for them. Feelings of insecurity in the first months of life lower levels of the mood-boosting chemicals serotonin and dopamine, and the effects are life-long, according to researchers.

Babies cry to communicate, and when you respond to their distress by cuddling and soothing them, you are teaching them that moods can be regulated and that they can recover from stress. This is an important lesson for later life. What's more, when stress hormones flood the brain, neural connections are eliminated. The brain fails to grow as quickly as it should.

Dr Stoppard and psychologist Dr Penelope Leach acknowledge that crying babies who do not get a response from their parents will eventually fall asleep—which is why this method has been promoted since the 1890s, and most famously in the 1980s by Dr Richard Ferber—but they do so defeated. Dr Leach told the *Guardian*:

> The reason babies raised on strict routine regimens go to sleep, usually with less and less crying, is because they are quicker and quicker to give up. Their brain has adapted to a world where they are not responded to.

Rather than leading babies to believe they are winning a pitched battle with their parents and encouraging calculated manipulation—something humans are not capable of until they are at least two years old—parents who respond to tears help their children develop new ways of expressing their needs, and they eventually end up crying less.

A popular alternative to 'cry it out' is 'verbal reassurance', which means that you pop your head in the door every five minutes while your baby is falling asleep to let them know you are there, deliver a few soothing words, and then return to your sofa and bucket of pinot gris. It is hard, because your baby will likely cry with heart-rending ululations and rather than picking them up and rocking them back to sleep as you would like to, you are advised to simply walk into baby's room, say something along the lines of, 'Time for sleep now, darling' and leave.

Verbal reassurance was the preferred method of the sleep-seminar woman, who had used it effectively with her many children. She advised that parents make sure their baby had everything in the cot required to get through the night comfortably, including one of several recommended and eye-wateringly expensive snugglies that looked like faceless octopi. It works, she assured us. Problems arise when you whip in there like a first class flight attendant and offer your baby a selection of items to make their journey to the Land of Nod as comfortable as possible: cuddles, bottle, boob, snuggly toy, dummy, story, blankie, lavender oil on the sheets, midnight story, you lying on the floor beside the cot like a body guard, lullabies, another story . . . (Please see: SUDI safe sleep guidelines, pg 225.)

In our own experience, verbal reassurance seemed to leave Micah angry and confused. He would stand in his cot, little arms reaching for us, and we would stand at the threshold of his room watching his distress, as if separated by a glass partition. Eventually he would fall asleep, but it could take hours and the process exhausted us all. And, still, he woke multiple times each night. We had to get tough.

For many families there comes a point, and you must judge this for yourself, when it is time to let your munchkin cry at night while you rest, content in the knowledge that they are secure, comfortable, well fed, and able to reach any one of the fifteen dummies you have sprinkled through their bedding. This is hard to believe when you have become accustomed to rising at 11 pm, 1 am, 3 am and 5 am to feed a hungry new-born, but by the time they are around six months old they no longer require a night-time feed to get them through to morning. And by the time they are nine to twelve months old they are not actually suffering when they cry at night, they are just looking for company. Unless, of course, they really are suffering from a fever or wet sheets, in which case their cry will have a different, easily identifiable pitch and you should, of course, respond.

We left our run for night-time freedom a bit late and consequently our little guy continued to remind us who was at the centre of our home by throwing his body against the bars of his cot at 3 am well after his first birthday, despite our introduction of the routines suggested by the sleep-seminar woman. And he would get so angry, crying for half an hour or more when we ignored him in the night. At eighteen months something switched in his little body and for a period of about two months he no longer woke in the night or, if he did, he managed to get himself back to sleep without any input from us. Developing an affection for a stuffed giraffe and teddy bear definitely helped, as he would loop one arm around each toy, stick his bum in the air, and snuggle down without a fuss.

And then without any apparent reason, the night-time

wakings began again. It was worse, I think, to return to the twilight zone after a period of reasonable sleep. We had become overconfident, staying up past 11 pm, standing outside his room and listening to his slow nocturnal breathing, toasting ourselves for making it through the sleepless months. When the 1 am, 3 am and 5 am wakings began anew we were more resentful, less soothing, more shouty.

We were not alone, as Dita, mother of two, explains:

I have found that when the kids were babies, I didn't mind getting up to feed them or comfort them. However, several years down the track and the patience certainly wears thin! And it seems getting up a few times at this stage is infinitely more tiring than the three-hour wake-up call when they were babies, for some reason.

We would leave Micah to cry—and cry—until one of us would jerk back the covers, stomp into his room and say, 'Micah! It's night-time. It's dark outside. Time for sleep.' And he would reply, 'Dark, go away! Go away, dark. Noooo!' We would threaten to take things away if he didn't lie down immediately: cars would be confiscated, visits with Granny rescinded. The results were uneven. Then I decided it was a technology problem—he must be knocking the sides of the cot as he slept and waking as a result. No wonder he was crying!

And so we installed the big-boy bed with great pomp and circumstance. We didn't herald its arrival with trumpets and banners but we may as well have, so hopeful were we that this would be the circuit breaker. Micah's big-boy bed really is big. It is a king single, which sounds oxymoronic, but really just means it is bigger than a standard single but smaller than a double. It is also quite high off the ground—when my mother saw it she could not hide her disapproval, even when we installed a set of bars to keep him in. It used to belong to his beloved cousin Walter and, as such, is endowed with tremendous mana.

I took Micah shopping and he chose a duvet cover stamped with silhouettes of cars, trucks, planes, helicopters and boats. He loves it. During the day he will walk into his room, point at his new furniture and say, 'Cool bed. Big boy.' We have made much of the fact that this wondrous new bed is only used for sleeping and reading bedtime stories. It is special. He is not to play on it. Scout is not to play on it. So when Micah is tired he sees it as a treat to be allowed to get into his cool big-boy bed. He will gather his bedtime buddies and march down the hallway calling, 'Night night. Night night.' To further seal the deal, we have instituted a homemade chart and sticker system. Every time Micah gets through the night without waking us, he gets a sticker for his chart—tiger, schnauzer, circus big top—and the fourth night, he gets a matchbox car, which makes him giggle with joy. Usually he prefers to wear his daily sticker on his stomach for a while and admire it, but eventually it goes up on his wall. For three months we have all slept properly—it feels like a miracle—but we aren't silly enough to think we have solved his sleeping aversion. This, too, could be a temporary fix.

Until you've been there, you can't quite imagine how challenging it is to look after a baby, run a house and organise yourself when you don't get enough sleep night after night, week after week, month after month for more than a year. Tim and I went 24 months without a proper sleep—and I could add another six months to my tally because pregnancy can mess with your slumber, too, and in my case it most assuredly did. So for two-and-a-half years I was a shell of myself, a pale and watery version of the woman formerly known as Eleanor. It's a ridiculous situation—yet common. Parents everywhere are stumbling through their daily routines and heading off to work, making decisions and running households without ever being truly rested. A lot of the time in my first year of motherhood I felt slightly drunk with fatigue and there were times when I chose not to drive because I didn't think I would be able to do so safely.

A survey by the British magazine *Mother and Baby* found that new mothers were surviving on less than four hours of sleep in 24 and were woken, on average, three times a night. Half of working mothers surveyed said their employers had been unsympathetic to their fatigue and 77 per cent admitted their tiredness was getting in the way of their work. In an ironic twist, many parents were getting so wound up about lack of sleep that their babies sensed their worry and refused to go to sleep. The editor of *Mother & Baby*, Elena Dalrymple, told the *Independent*:

Today's working parents are so time-poor their anxiety to get baby to bed so they can have a bit of an evening actually prevents baby from falling asleep. Babies latch on to their parents' anxiety and stay awake instead.

The effects of sleep deprivation, while blackly comic, are serious and include low mood, irritability, low sex drive, emotional outbursts, difficulty thinking clearly and a sense that every task is harder than it should be. Sleep allows the body to refresh itself after a busy day, and REM (rapid eye movement) sleep, when we dream, allows the brain to process the events of the day. If you don't get enough REM sleep you start forgetting what happened just yesterday, and that's an awful feeling. It's as though you are living underwater—everything is blurry and feels heavy and odd. You struggle with simple, familiar tasks and anything added to your day's agenda, say a trip to the doctor with a coughing baby, or a flat tyre, feels like a crisis.

Good sleep isn't just about the number of hours slumber you manage to clock up in 24, it's about the quality of sleep, too, according to a study published in the *American Journal of Obstetrics and Gynaecology*. Being woken often by a crying baby has a similar effect on new parents as the disorder sleep apnoea, in which a sufferer wakes often due to breathing abnormalities. Researcher Dr Hawley Montgomery-Downs from West Virginia University explained that sleep occurs in cycles lasting 90 minutes to two hours. If a mother is woken often enough, she may not get through any full sleep cycles in a night, leaving her unrefreshed.

Sleep deprivation was such a problem for mother-of-twins, Sarah, that it put her off having more children, and

I must admit it has given me cause to pause, too. Joanna, mother of two, explains:

Lack of sleep in the early days definitely made everything rougher—I overreacted to small things and misplaced items like the car keys even more often than usual. I also remember getting a kitchen burn on my arm and it got infected so I had to go to White Cross one weekend. The doctor told me it was because I was so tired and rundown that my body had allowed the infection to develop. I remember being amazed he didn't actually ask further questions, to see how I was coping. I was fine, just pushing too hard, but what if I hadn't been okay?

Jane, mother of two, struggled with two poor sleepers:

Our solution was to buy double beds for the kids—they came out of cots and into double beds. Then at least when they woke, one of us could just climb in with whichever child had woken, whisper sweet nothings and then resume sleep. I remember my husband saying, 'It's like living at Buckingham Palace in our house. You never know which bed you will wake up in!'

In the two years that we struggled with Micah's night-time habits, friends pushed several popular books into my hands with those golden words: 'I found this really helpful.' I hadn't read much of Gina Ford's *The Contented Little Baby Book* before

I realised her approach wasn't for me. Who was this woman, the White Witch of Narnia? Where was her compassion? I couldn't stick to that kind of punishing schedule and I couldn't bear to try and make my baby bend to her will. There were charts and checklists and a growly section on the soppiness of demand feeding, which was my chosen path. According to Ms Ford I had failed my baby before we even left the hospital by not getting him into a sleep-and-feed routine. Pah!

Tracy Hogg, the self-styled 'baby whisperer' annoyed me with her syrupy tone. She wasn't my nanny for pity's sake, and why did she insist on addressing me as 'Mum'? But I did like the way she broke down the day into four easily identifiable parts: EASY: Eat, Activity, Sleep and You. That 'You' meant me, the mother, having some golden time to myself. The problem was I never seemed to make it to that fourth part of the cycle. It was all EAS at our house.

On Becoming Baby Wise: Giving Your Infant the Gift of Night-time Sleep by Gary Ezzo and Robert Bucknam bored me rigid—each chapter ended with 'questions for review' like a text book. No thanks. I found *Sleep: The Easy Way to Peaceful Nights* by Beatrice Hollyer and Lucy Smith, which spoke of the 'core night'—the number of hours a baby is able to sleep uninterrupted each night, which you build on until you have twelve of them strung in a row like precious beads—too complicated for my sleep-starved brain. It did, however, help a friend get both her babies onto a sensible schedule within weeks of their arrival.

Sleep gurus are goddesses in this sleep-deprived climate—an estimated 25 per cent of us do not get enough rest, and parents are passionate about anyone who can deliver it to them. I have heard emotional stories about the bliss of handing a sleepless infant over to a nurse and climbing into bed at the Plunket Family Centre. 'It saved my life,' a friend told me.

As a culture, we seem to be particularly exercised by the inconvenience of babies who are unreliable sleepers, and much of the received wisdom is contradictory. As Fiona, mother of two, points out:

> There is so much advice around now about attachment and the importance of being responsive and attuned which I absolutely agree with, but I do think that sometimes the message gets carried to the extreme, where parents are made to feel that they will irreparably damage their child if they let them cry for an instant, and so they lift and soothe so much that the baby never gets to learn how to fall asleep independently.

It is worth noting if you have a sleep-averse baby that every child's brain is wired differently and there is no parenting advice or solution that is going to work for every family. Also, as several hardened parents told me, no five-year-old is bouncing out of bed five times a night. They will learn to sleep with time. This hazy, exhausting period won't last forever.

Even now that Micah has got his night-time sleeps down, he is a patchy and unreliable napper. While most babies will take two naps a day into their eighteenth month, he dropped his second sleep by ten months, settling on one sleep of 45 minutes to three hours duration (on rare and auspicious days), starting at any time from 10.30 am to 2 pm. It can be hard to plan your day around this moving target, and planning around my son has never been a strength of mine, consequently Micah is often dragged around town rubbing his eyes and asking for his bottle. The alternative is for us to stay home all day, and for me that is no alternative at all. The way I see it, Micah gets a good rest every day and doesn't seem to be suffering any ill effects of our unorthodox system. Some toddlers, if they get a daytime sleep, will stay up till 10 pm. Their parents may prefer to cut out the nap in favour of a bedtime early enough to allow them an evening to themselves.

And what of me? Well, I often lie down and have a snooze when Micah does and these kips allow me to function. On waking I chugalug a cup of coffee and a biscuit or two and I'm good to go. I'd rather I could manage without these sleeps, that Micah was a more predictable kid, and that I could get on top of this 'routine' business but our way of coping works for us and when it doesn't work any longer, I'm sure we'll figure out some new way of doing things. I am tired of anguishing about it. I am tired in general.

The truth is, you will suffer some level of sleep deprivation when you have a baby, even if you have a well-established routine. Sometimes your baby will be sick, or distressed, or simply peeved that you wouldn't let him watch Elmo all night, and sleep will not happen. So how can you make the best of it? Here are my tips for exhausted mothers (and fathers):

* Form a napping habit as quickly as you can, not just for baby. Take little hits of sleep whenever you can, or if you can't fall asleep lie down with a book. At least your body will be resting.
* Take a brisk walk. Fresh air and a bit of exercise really can make you feel better, even if the prospect of putting on your trainers and settling baby in the pram seems too complicated. It's worth it. Start with five minutes and work upwards from there.
* Take a shower and use yummy bath gel to revive your senses.
* Eat good food: slow-release carbohydrates, like wholemeal bread, banana and porridge, and iron-rich foods, like red meat and leafy greens give energy.
* Try not to drink too much coffee and tea. Excess caffeine in your system makes it harder for you to take advantage of those little windows of opportunity that open up for afternoon naps. It also can make it harder to fall asleep at night. If breastfeeding, it can also lead to a restless, grizzly baby that won't sleep. I failed to follow this advice myself, spectacularly, but apparently it really helps.
* Be kind to yourself. Don't try to fit too much into each day. The world is not going to tilt on its axis if you don't get around to the laundry today, or tomorrow.

Further reading

On Becoming Baby Wise: Giving Your Infant the Gift of Night-time Sleep by Gary Ezzo and Robert Buckman, Parent-Wise Solutions, 2006

Secrets of the Baby Whisperer, by Tracy Hogg with Melinda Blan, Ballantine Books, 2001

Sleep: The Easy Way to Peaceful Nights by Beatrice Hollyer and Lucy Smith, Cassell Illustrated, 2002

The Contented Little Baby Book by Gina Ford, New American Library, 2001

'Babies Left to Cry Can Suffer Brain Damage, Warns Parenting Guru' by Sarah Cassidy, *The Independent*, 22 April 2010

'Should We Leave Babies to Cry?' *The Independent* 9 June 2009

'The Crying Game' by Peter Feeney, *North and South*, September 2007

'How to Get Kids to Sleep More' by Ashley Merryman, *New York*, 7 October 2007

'New Moms Get Enough Sleep, Just Not Good Sleep' by Amy Norton, 30 August 2010 at reuters.com

7. Those blasted mummy wars

In which stay-at-home mothers are pitched against working mothers and no-one wins

Lisa, a stay-at-home mother of two, describes what it is really like being at home with preschoolers:

> Some people think being at home is like having a holiday and that you have all this spare time. In reality, being a mum is a hundred times harder than my job before I had kids. Mums these days are expected to be superwoman: look after the kids, be a domestic goddess and work as well. Something has to give.

Elise, a working mother of two, talks about her return to work:

> I had to go back to work to take the pressure off our large mortgage. I've been told if I chose to have

children, I should be with them for the first three years, or what's the point? I returned to work full time when my son was nine months and I will return to work again after my daughter reaches ten months. I have to say, getting back to work made me feel human again. It was nice to use my brain and meet new people. I think it's made me a better mum as my son is happy, healthy and learning lots and when I pick him up, I have all the time in the world for him as I've missed him during the day and want to be with him 150 per cent.

When Micah was a year old I decided to dip my toes in the world of work again, giddy with the idea that I could start and complete tasks on the same day. Honestly, I think I was looking for a way out of my lounge. Another month at home, playing hostage to an adorable little boy in stretch Levis— 'Mo-ah, mo-ah' was his constant demand . . . more food, more music, more cuddles, more stories, more attention now, now, now—and I might have lost the will to get out of bed.

As a writer I was lucky to have the experience and contacts that allowed me to work from home, even if that simply meant reviewing a few books and writing the odd magazine story. Once Micah was over breastfeeding and my brain was sharper, I took on more challenging stories and worked the occasional day in the office. I attempted to achieve that elusive goal: work–life balance, which I had long suspected was a crock of caca conceived by magazine writers, in the same category as anti-cellulite diets and quizzes that purported to diagnose your relationship problems. Did I manage it? Not sure yet, but

I feel a thousand times better for trying. It turns out—and this surprised no-one who knew me—that I was not a natural fit for staying at home full time despite my best efforts and my fervent belief that it was the best thing for my son.

I felt claustrophobic and slightly desperate each morning when I dropped my husband off at the train station. He was heading somewhere with lunch breaks and adult conversation and hours of uninterrupted internet trawling. I was returning to the sour comforts of our lounge, where racks of teeny singlets and babygros were drying in front of the heater, and where I would spend many fruitless hours trying to convince my little guy to take a nap so I could get some rest too.

That is my experience. I know women who have thrown themselves into home life with enthusiasm and skill, who combine play dates and errands with scheduled nap times and domestic duties with elan. That is their experience. There are, as with most situations in life, pros and cons on both sides. I'm not sure why women then have to stake out their battle lines and wage 'war' with each other over these very personal choices. It is an anti-sisterhood response to an experience that, frankly, kicks everyone's butt. No matter what choice you make, you will question yourself. That is the nature of motherhood.

Psychologist Oliver James summarises the issue in his book *How Not To F*** Them Up*, about how to best care for the under-threes. He says working mothers in Britain and the United States (and by logical extension, Australia and New Zealand) are torn between the cultural belief that babies need 'omnipresent loving care', ideally provided by the mother, and the high value placed on financial success and material wealth which is very hard to achieve on one income. Stay-at-home mothers are comforted by the cultural belief that they should follow their instincts when caring for their child but are bombarded with 'expert' advice and media depictions of motherhood which do not necessarily jibe with their own experiences.

As a result, says James, mothers on both sides of the divide tend to stereotype each other. Home-based mothers assume their working counterparts are 'denying their natural tendencies' while secretly wishing they too could stay at home. Not only that, stay-at-home mothers often characterise working mothers as neglectful and cold, says James. Working mothers are supposedly less critical of stay-at-home mothers, and feel unfairly maligned, although Western culture is, in the main, supportive of working mothers, and stay-at-home mothers are far less common after the baby's first year of life.

In New Zealand, where most mothers end up doing some form of paid work, we still idealise the home-based mother, according to Jane Harrison, whose doctoral thesis examined the role of mothers in modern Kiwi society. In 'Negotiating Motherhood Identity: Representations, Resistance and Regulation' she wrote that there is a pervasive societal belief that women who leave their children in the care of others for more than short periods are bad mothers. Mothers she interviewed who put their children into care so they could work or study felt guilty about it:

Not only did these women feel inadequate as mothers if they left their children in childcare institutions for too long, they also perceived the quality of their interactions with their children when they were with them as crucial to the child's ongoing development and emotional well being.

This, unsurprisingly, led to heightened stress and worry. As Linda, a mother of one, told me:

> I did once read something by Erica Jong saying it was fine to have your baby taken care of for the first couple of years so you could get on with your career, but I found going back to work was very tough, even with an excellent daycare facility.

Pick up a mothering magazine or browse an online mothering forum and you will find an avalanche of concern over childcare choices and the effect a working mother has on the family. For a woman who is heading back to work after taking maternity leave it is frightening. And that's before you factor in the advice she will be getting from acquaintances and colleagues, her own self doubt, and her family's assessment of her choice.

Anneliese, a mother of three, runs a small business and was keen to get back to work as soon as practically possible after the births of her children:

> My mother would make comments about me not being at home with the kids, even when [my husband] was—'It's not the same as having a mother at home,' she'd

say. The kids' difficult behaviour was—and still is—rationalised by her as them not spending enough time with their mother. Of course if they did spend all their time with their mother I would probably end up beating them out of sheer frustration!

Mother-of-one and businesswoman Sonia copped an earful from other mothers when she went back to work and hired a full-time nanny. But as she explains:

Other people rely on me to pay their wages and to keep the company running. I don't have a normal nine to five job where I can just leave for twelve months and then go back part time. I would have to shut the business down if I did. Why can't I have both?

Mother-of-one Helen gets tired of people asking her who looks after her daughter when she works:

I had one person who was actually a client of mine go on about it and how she hoped I didn't come to regret giving it up, but I just don't feel like that and what's right for me may not be right for them. I don't criticise them for their decisions—it's up to them!

Part-time work, often offered as a panacea for women who fear they are losing career traction or simply want some regular adult company, is not without its problems either. A University of Canterbury report on implementing

family-friendly work practices—'Whose Role Is It Anyway?',
by Susan Lilley—found that employers' attitudes to part-time
work varied widely:

> One perception of part-time work is that it offers
> the best of both worlds. However, studies show that
> part-time work may or may not be family friendly
> depending on the circumstances in which it is offered.

Given a workplace culture that favours long hours, someone
who ducks out early to pick up the kids can be seen as less
reliable and less serious about career advancement than her
colleagues. This can be incredibly galling for someone who by
the time she has children may have spent fifteen years build-
ing a career she enjoys and derives enormous satisfaction
from. Not to mention that it is probably a necessity for helping
with mortgage or rent payments and supermarket bills.

There is evidence in the United States that mothers who
would like a role in the workplace are being forced out by
employer inflexibility, workplace bias against mothers, and
a lack of family support. The report '"Opt Out" or Pushed
Out?: How the Press Covers Work/Family Conflict', from the
Center for Worklife Law, University of California, Hastings
College of the Law, suggests that, while there have been news
stories for the past ten years reporting on the trend for mothers to opt out of the workplace in favour of child-rearing,
women are *not* choosing this path. Rather, they are being
forced to take it. The report states:

The ideal worker is still someone who starts to work in early adulthood and works, full time and full force for forty years straight. That means no time off for child-bearing. Or child-rearing.

The authors cite studies in which women are said to have taken career 'off-ramps' only to find it is more difficult to re-enter the workforce than they'd expected—and they want it more than they expected.

In this part of the world, where we share many social conditions and attitudes with the famously sensible Scandinavian countries, we enjoy far more workplace flexibility than in the United States, but that doesn't mean we can afford to be complacent. Equally, we shouldn't make women who genuinely choose to stay at home feel like conservative throw-backs. A fed-up member of ohbaby.co.nz said that she pretended she wanted to go back to work more than she actually did in order to fit in:

Some of my high-flying friends were really shocked when I resigned. I actually think there's heaps of pressure for mums to go back to work.

She gets the sense from others that she might be selling herself short by staying home with her children and while she doesn't believe this herself, she is troubled by the implications.

Although many mothers idealise the stay-at-home scenario, it can be tedious and hard on a woman's self-esteem. As Shan, mother of two, explains:

I have found career-prioritising mothers almost invariably patronising and sometimes downright rude to stay-at-home mothers—some out of genuine scorn, others I think because they feel guilty about the time they are not spending with their own children. I have had many women question what on earth I do with myself all day—everything they are paying three different people to do—and also unwanted commentary on finances: 'Oh, I just couldn't bear not having my own money to spend', for example. My husband is the earner in our household, but I'm busting a gut raising our children, so as far as I am concerned—and as far as he is concerned—I am earning every penny that he brings home as much as he is.

Anna found it hard to deal with the assumption that she would, as a matter of course, return to work after a brief period of maternity leave:

No one, except my grandmother, said words to the effect of 'Good on you for making the sacrifices necessary to stay at home'. Instead, it seemed many people thought I was opting for the easy route when actually, for me, the easy route would've been going back to work, to a job I loved, instead of staying home with a refluxy baby. Maybe I was being oversensitive but I would hear it in comments like, 'So what else are you doing with yourself?' Or my father-in-law, calling in the morning: 'Have you been outside to sunbathe yet?' I don't blame them—most people just have no idea, or have forgotten, what it's like to care for a baby and when they're working a full-time job, 'trapped' at a desk, the idea of staying at home with a baby may seem idyllic.

Mother-of-three Gillian is tired of justifying her choice to stay at home:

Actually, if you really want to know, I struggle to just cope with my three kids and some sort of order in the house let alone cope with the organisation necessary to cater for a job, after school activities, homework, sick children, school holidays and a husband that has a highly demanding job with odd hours. I am also concerned that I need to show my daughters that underneath it all I believe that women can have careers and that their father and I have a partnership. We discussed early on that we wanted someone at home to look after the kids when they were young and he has a personality that is ambitious and career-driven so the natural choice was me.

The result of Mummy-Wars finger-pointing and defensiveness is that often stay-at-home mothers and working mothers mix about as well as oil and water. Each feels that the other does not understand them, or is judging them in some way. Mothers overcompensate for perceived weaknesses, and misunderstandings are added to, rather than overcome. Working mother-of-two Catherine says:

I never felt that comfortable in some of the play groups that I tried when the kids were little. Because I am career-oriented and always did a little bit of work even when they were babies, I felt almost inadequate around the stay-at-home mums who made that their life purpose. It felt that conversations were only about children and, while I love my kids more than life itself, I find life interesting and enjoy conversations about all types of things. Because I actually don't really care about Tupperware, I find it hard sometimes being with mums who have structured their life around their children and their home life—and that does manifest in feeling guilty and inadequate because am I meant to feel fulfilled by staying at home and having a perfectly organised pantry?

On the other hand, Jackie, mother of two, looks back with the benefit of hindsight and says:

I've learned over the years that being an at-home mum is the best, most valuable job you can do. I put my kids into daycare and went back to work because I thought that was what I was supposed to do—that I should be contributing more. If I had that time again I would simply have learned to manage our money better so that I didn't have to go out to work and could stay at home with my kids instead. As it is, I think I took home about $10 a week for working 30 hours after petrol and child-care expenses. But women have fought for generations for more rights and more independence. These days we can do it all, and sadly I think many of us feel that's exactly what we have to do, rather than simply focusing on our kids.

Catherine sees the issue quite differently:

I want to be a role model to my children that you can have a purpose in life, that you can make a difference in the world and that you should feel fulfilled in what you do. My secret horror is the life half lived.

The trade-off for enjoying her career is lashings of guilt: for being away from home so much, for ditching work to attend daycare parties, for not being there when her children are unwell. Particularly keen for her is the guilt she feels when she is away with work for the second night in a row and, talking to her daughter via video chat on her laptop, her daughter says, 'Mummy I want you to come home right now'. She also says:

When I have been woken at 1 am with a sick child with a high temperature and I have to leave the house at 5:30 am to catch that early plane to travel to run a workshop that I can't cancel, leaving my husband to look after my sick child—those plane trips when you can't answer your phone when you know you have a sick child and are wondering what on earth is going on, are just horrendous.

I have decided to give up on my feelings of inadequacy around stay-at-home mums—I know that I would not cope with that lifestyle, and I do know that I have happy, healthy kids that I spend copious amounts of quality time with—they will go for weeks without watching TV or a DVD, whereas when I was at home with them that was much more common when I needed a break.

When you talk to women about the work-vs-home issue, the emotion is barely contained. They are angry and frustrated, and rightly so:

* Giving up a treasured job to parent is tough.
* Working long hours when you would rather be with your baby is tough.
* Being pushed out of the workplace because you need more flexibility than your employer can provide is tough.
* Realising, like Jackie did, that a week's work barely covers childcare expenses, let alone providing extra cash for the family, is tough.
* Being criticised for your choices is beyond the pale.

There are no easy answers, just a lot of women—and men—trying to do their best. The right compromise for each family is unique to that family. Unfortunately, many families are not satisfied with the arrangement that they have and the compromises they have had to make. Ministry of Social Development research found one-third of households in which both parents work wished one partner could stay home. The *Work, Family and Parenting* report for the ministry also concluded that more than 50 per cent of parents work overtime at least once a week and nearly 50 per cent take work home. More than one-third of parents surveyed said their work schedule interfered with family life at least once a week. Twenty per cent of working parents reported a lot of work-related stress and just under half admitted they lost their temper with their children as a result.

Either way, there are frustrations, as Anna, mother of two, explains:

> I was raised to be and do everything a boy could do, to be an achiever—and now I am barefoot in the kitchen, making dinner, folding washing . . . yet some biological urge prevents me from opting for the opposite—leaving my child with a stranger and going back to work full-time. I've tried for part-time work but haven't had any luck. So sometimes I feel a little trapped.

Mother of three Vanessa Mealings told the *New Zealand Herald* she was facing childcare charges of $800 a week and was considering working nights and weekends so she could leave the children with her partner instead. She said:

> That will be a pretty big strain on Scott being at home with three little kids at night by himself and a strain for me finishing work early morning and then getting up at whatever time the kids get up—but it's the only way that's feasible for me to come back to work.

So, while the fact that parents are struggling to merge work and child-rearing is hardly news, we still haven't been able to produce an agreed solution on what to do with the children who need to be cared for while their parents are away from home. It seems almost irresponsible to suggest that there is one ideal path and most experts will say that—within reason—whatever works best for the mother is best for the children, because contented, engaged mothers raise contented, secure children. But of course, it's not as simple as that.

There are some known variables. Children under the age of three are happiest and most secure with a trusted, loved caregiver. That person need not be a parent, but does need to be immediately responsive to the child's requirements. Even when a child is in a childcare situation, it is preferable to have a primary caregiver on whom they can rely to meet their basic needs and offer comfort when required. Ideally, this person is their go-to adult while they are at the childcare centre and a treasured member of the child's group of trusted adults.

The childcare environment should be much like the home, according to UNICEF, which advocates for children and raises funds for children's aid. The organisation's report on childcare in the OECD, 'The Childcare Transition', says:

> The available research is consistent in finding that the quality of early childhood education and care depends above all else on the ability of the caregiver to build relationships with children and to provide a secure, consistent, sensitive, stimulating and rewarding

environment. In other words, good childcare is an extension of good parenting.

As to when it is acceptable to put a child into formalised care, the UNICEF report avoids any conclusion:

> The question of the appropriate age at which early childhood education and care can be of benefit to children is one of the most controversial issues in the childcare debate.

But others do not hedge their bets on this topic. In response to the UNICEF report, New Zealand paediatrician and former Children's Commissioner, Dr Ian Hassall, said:

> We are engaged in a massive uncontrolled experiment that has already largely transferred the care of three- to five-year-olds to non-family members for a good proportion of their waking hours and is in the process of doing the same for younger children. We should take a rational look at this and ask ourselves if it's good for children and their families . . . While the trend has strong roots in family economics, women's self-realisation, national productivity and consumerism as well as the desire to advance the development of our children we shouldn't regard it as inevitable and should realise that we can adopt public policy options that either encourage or discourage it.

In other words, this is a Government-level issue and deserves more attention. UNICEF New Zealand domestic advocacy manager Barbara Lambourn said:

> While the trend towards early childhood education and care can help give older children the best possible start in life and boost educational achievement, it is worrying to see increasing numbers of children under three years of age being cared for in groups outside the home.

And Children's Commissioner John Angus says that while toddlers benefit from the social interaction and learning opportunities provided by childcare centres, the under-twos need close attachment to adults and just one or two carers. He told a group of graduating New Zealand teachers in 2010:

> It is a fundamentally important period in a child's development and there are different risks to manage about infection, affiliation and attachment, and about stress.

Australian psychologist Steve Biddulph questions whether children under the age of three should even be in childcare, given their preference for 'one special person' to look after them. He has written a book on the subject, *Raising Babies: Why Your Love is Best*.

Whether or not it is ideal, however, many parents do put their children into care before they turn three. According to the OECD, New Zealand families pay 28 per cent of their net income towards childcare, placing us fourth highest out of 32 member countries. (The OECD average is just thirteen per cent.) Like it or not, institutional childcare is part of the equation for many small children. So how do you make the best childcare choice you can for your child? Anecdotally, you would wonder if the options for early childcare are adequate, let alone exceptional—and not just at early childcare centres. Every mother you speak to, it seems, has worried about the standard of care available and whether it is good enough for her child. I remember the sinking feeling when I visited a gym I was considering joining, baby in tow. While I was impressed by the shiny equipment and tanned, buff staff, I was most interested in the creche. I was speechless when faced with a barred cubicle system in which babies were stowed while parents hit the stair climber and leg push. Any child unable to walk was put in one of these little baby cages for the duration of their stay. I could not figure out what to say about this, and I never returned.

When choosing childcare, parents can use guidelines provided by the Ministry of Education. There is also a New Zealand Childcare Association which aims to improve the standard of childcare and education, and concerns itself with identifying best practice.

According to UNICEF, the benchmarks for successful early childhood education include at least 80 per cent of staff who have significant contact with children—including home-based care—getting relevant training. At least half of staff should have a minimum of three years tertiary education or a recognised early childhood qualification. The minimum ratio of children to trained staff for centres looking after four- and five-year-olds should be fifteen to one, and the total group should not exceed 24 children.

Underpinning everything is the benchmark that New Zealand has failed to achieve: a minimum entitlement to paid parental leave of one year at 50 per cent of salary. Instead, in New Zealand the minimum paid parental leave is fourteen weeks at 50 per cent, and that puts us at the bottom of the OECD league table, with just the United States faring worse. Australia was also in the sin bin until recently, when it introduced paid parental leave at the minimum wage for up to eighteen weeks.

The lack of good, flexible childcare options is a huge barrier for women who want to work, and those stay-at-home mothers who would like a break every now and then. With the deterioration of the traditional family structure, in which elders would care for small children while parents provided food and shelter, we are forced to pay someone to look after our precious ones, and that is a daunting prospect. If you find yourself needing a childcare centre, do your research. Ask everyone you know if they have used or heard of an exceptional centre. Visit any centre that grabs your interest and ask lots of questions—don't worry, they're used to it. Finally, the Education Review Office, which assesses all primary and secondary schools in New Zealand, also reports on childcare centres. Go to ero.govt. nz and search the centres you are interested in.

Workplaces also have a responsibility towards working mothers and need to become more flexible, as Anna, mother of two, explains:

Workplaces have to adjust to work around mothers. Originally, men went to work and women stayed at home with the children. Then, after a couple of world wars and the feminist movement, women joined men at work, and workplaces haven't adapted accordingly. Workplaces should offer more flexible working options. Law changes requiring workplaces to offer staff flexible working options have helped, but I am told many are still adjusting to the changes.

I was able to stay home with my son for the first year of his life because my husband earned enough to house and feed us, and because we had committed to a simpler lifestyle. *That last bit is critical.* This is what we do:

* We share a car.
* We make do with what we already own.
* When we do spend our money, we buy quality furniture and home wares that last.
* We no longer eat out often, or go to the movies, or go on overseas holidays.
* We pay off the credit card every month.
* We don't buy things we can't afford.
* We dress Micah in hand-me-downs and limit the number of toys we give him.

We're not Quakers or hippies, we just learned to live with less. For us, it has been worth it. That doesn't mean I wasn't excited to get back to work and earn money. I was. But I chose a part-time position that means Micah is in daycare just two days a week, and for our family that's enough. We are also lucky that we have an energetic grandmother on hand, which many families aren't fortunate enough to have.

For me, full-time at-home mothering proved to be a gloomy choice. This was a revelation, as I had assumed it would allow me loads of time to read books and learn to cook interesting and impressive meals. I knew small babies slept a lot and I envisaged using that time to learn, once and for all, how to make a stir-fry that wasn't overpowered by the salty notes of fish sauce, and to finally finish Vikram Seth's doorstop novel, *A Suitable Boy*. I didn't realise that when the baby sleeps, you are wise to take a nap yourself, or suffer the consequences. When I discovered how vile I was without those naps, I took to them with gusto.

Besides the isolation, the worst part of that year at home for me—and judging from my research, not just for me but for many mums—was all the ruddy cleaning. This sounds trite but believe me, it becomes a placard-waving issue when you're stuck doing it every day—and we know from many research studies that even when women are working outside the home they end up getting lumped with the lion's share of cleaning jobs. When you're not changing a nappy, soothing your tot, or inventing new diversions for him, you clean as if your life depends on it, wiping surfaces over and over until your hands dry up and your cuticles bleed. That is until your baby is at the stage where everything goes into her mouth, when you convince yourself that a bit of dog hair on the carpet will aid immunity.

I have always been a clean person if not a tidy one. (My mother tells me I was a snap to toilet train because I didn't want to mess up my frilly undies.) While I hate food shopping I enjoy choosing cleaning products, with scent being a major selling point. It pleases me to see pristine sponges and unopened bottles of dish-washing liquid in the cupboard under the sink. But when you work outside the home you can keep a certain distance between yourself and your Jif. One good clean once a week does the business.

When I was at home every day I couldn't ignore the sticky residue on the stove top or the soap scum on the bathroom vanity. And, if you're like me, you will find that it plagues you, too, so you will feel compelled to do something about it. The next thing you know you're slathering the richest L'Occitane moisturiser (a luxurious pre-baby gift you'd never feel comfortable buying for yourself) into your hands every night to counteract the effects of orange-scented Spray 'n' Wipe—and they will still feel like the finest sandpaper.

While that's fairly dispiriting, even worse is the fact that, despite your best efforts, the house doesn't actually look that good. Children come with stuff, masses of it. Detritus moves around the house, seemingly at will—dummies, muslins, hats and socks, rattles, books, partially drained bottles of milk, toilet rolls and receipts from your handbag—attaching itself to shelving units and sideboards and tables. It drives me absolutely bonkers. Unwilling to give in to the mess, I shuffle sleepily from room to room with a Chux in hand like one of the undead.

Turns out I aspire to have a home worthy of a spread in

my favourite housekeeping magazine, *Your Home and Garden*, to which I recently subscribed. You know the family homes of which I speak: warm and inviting, casual yet polished, rich in New Zealand art and good literature and European electronics. The children who inhabit these homes have names like Maximillian and Cheyenne and play with cool wooden toys that are as stylish as they are educational. The family dogs, and there is usually at least one, do not shed or bring mud into the house. Spending the day in one of those homes would be an absolute pleasure, a mini-vacation, and not a jot like a day at ours.

But I don't envy those people, I simply find their existence comforting. Someone out there is living the life I thought I'd lead—it is possible, maybe.

I have a housework-averse friend whose personal philosophy is 'Get out, stay out'. If she's not at home to see the mess, she can't be expected to clean it, she says, and you can't argue with her logic. With a small child, I am not as mobile as my friend, though I have given it my best shot. The problem is, when I come home after an hour or two commiserating with other mothers, or now that I am working, from a day writing headlines, the mess reaches out and smacks me on the nose. It won't be ignored and I can't relax until I've whizzed round the kitchen with my squirt bottle.

I am trying to get over myself. I am re-reading *The I Hate to Housekeep Book* by Peg Bracken, an American home hints guru with a gloriously sloppy attitude. First published in 1962, it contains comforting chapters such as 'Dinner Will Be Ready As Soon as I Decide What We're Having', 'How to be Happy

When You're Absolutely Miserable' and 'The Hostess With the Leastest', which I aspire to one day be.

The chapter 'Don't Just Do Something, Sit There' ends thus:

> If you put your mind to it, and play your cards right, there are a great many things you don't have to do. Things could be worse, much worse, and let us all remember that, and count our blessings.'

Amen, Ms Bracken.

Further reading

How Not to F*** Them Up by Oliver James, Vermillion, June 2010

Mommy Wars: Stay-at-Home and Career Moms Face Off on Their Choices, Their Lives and Their Families edited by Leslie Morgan Steiner, Random House, 2006

The I Hate to Housekeep Book: When and How to Keep House Without Losing Your Mind by Peg Bracken, Arlington Books, 1962

'Costs make return to work hardly worthwhile' by Elizabeth Binning, *New Zealand Herald*, 22 March 2011

'Motherhood, Employment and the "Child Penalty"' by Maureen Baker, Women's Studies International Forum, Volume 33, Issue 3, University of Auckland, May–June 2010

'Blue is the New Black' by Maureen Dowd, *New York Times*, 19 September 2009

'Motherhood "Devastates" Women's Pay, Research Finds' by Amelia Gentleman, *The Guardian*, 10 July 2009

'UNICEF, The Childcare Transition, Innocenti Report Card 8', The United Nations Children's Fund, 2008

'"Oh!" Said a Competitive Mum When She Discovered Where We Lived. "The Third World . . ."' by Kate Murray, *The Independent*, 2 September 2006

'Work, Family and Parenting' by Colmar Brunton for Centre for Social Research and Evaluation, Ministry of Social Development, 2006

'Whose Role Is It Anyway?: Implementing Family Friendly Workplace Practices in New Zealand' Susan Lilley, University of Canterbury, 2004

'Negotiating Motherhood Identity: Representations, Resistance and Regulation' by Jane Harrison, University of Canterbury, 2003

'The Opt-Out Revolution' by Lisa Belkin, *New York Times*, 26 October 2003

'Babies and Bosses: Balancing Work and Family Life', Organisation for Economic Cooperation and Development at oecd.org, July 2008

Ministry of Education guidelines for choosing early childhood education centre at minedu.govt.nz/Parents/AllAges/ECEListing.aspx

Social and Demographic Trends, Pew Research Centre, 1 October 2009

Women's Work, The Washington Post at washingtonpost.com HD Video Podcast, 15 April 2007

8. Mothering in the 21st century

Life is supposed to be easier now, so why doesn't it
feel easier?

Motherhood is still considered the 'natural' state for New
Zealand women. The vast majority of fertile women, if you
ask them, will tell you that if they don't already have children
they expect that one day they will. It's just what we do. As a
society we celebrate motherhood as the 'right' choice, and in
a small island nation needing to rethink the way it distributes
its labour force—and, indeed, what the leading industries
should be—having children is seen as an economically positive thing to do.

So most women entering motherhood feel supported, and
if they are honest, at least a little gleeful that they are joining
the big girls' club and will *finally* have something to say at
dinner parties when talk turns to family and school zones.

Pregnancy news is greeted with gasps of pleasure and
enormous hugs and a barrage of questions about dates and

names and decorating bedrooms. Baby's arrival is met with balloons and flowers and jokes about getting busy producing a little brother or sister (closely followed by exasperated eye-rolling on the part of the new mother). If you are lucky, you will get a couple of nights in hospital, where nurses will teach you how to bathe your baby, how to change a nappy and how to breastfeed, and then you'll be sent home with a quick lesson in how to strap baby into the car seat. This will coincide neatly with the onset of third-day baby blues.

Fatigue, fear that you will do something wrong, and the sheer weird adjustment of having a tiny, mewling creature in the house will combine into a nasty little cloud of self doubt: you will crash, you will cry, and with time and help you will get over it.

The effects of the baby blues can be minimised. If you are feeling low, try the following:

* Eat a well-balanced diet
* Talk to your partner, family and friends
* Exercise—a stroll around the block will do
* Maintain realistic expectations of yourself.

Rebecca, who had her first child at 38, recalls her experience:

Although I had many friends and two sisters with children, I don't think anything can prepare you for the extreme tiredness and often relentless nature of being a mum. Not to mention the endless worry of first time motherhood—are they too hot; are they hungry; if they sleep too long, are they still breathing; everyone else's baby is crawling, why isn't mine? There is no let up, and while you might get the odd break, it's not till they are a lot older that you get to really have some time to yourself, or with your partner or friends.

For Rebecca the daily shower became a treasured time-out, a window of sanity:

Having a shower was a godsend as it helped set me up for the day and was a piece of time just for me.

If that sounds ridiculous to you, wait until you get there, sister. My advice: invest in a couple of nice, fragrant bath gels so you can make the most of your three minutes of alone time each morning—that daily ritual is like gold dust.

A hundred and fifty years ago women in New Zealand didn't ease into a day of intense mothering with a nice hot shower infused with the scent of grapefruit and geranium. Back then, she wouldn't even have imagined the joy of pushing a pram to a favourite cafe for a life-giving latte; it was unlikely that childcare duties were shared by fathers; and there were few shiny appliances or cleaning services or childcare professionals to ease a mother's workload. Nor could she expect any gratitude for fulfilling her 'God-given function'.

On the other hand, there was no expectation that she would keep up with a career; return to pre-pregnancy form; educate her babies; entertain her brood; and ensure their social status by throwing the best birthday parties with the biggest goodie bags—all to be done with a modest smile. Mothering, like everything else in life, is affected by trends and social conditions. When early Maori women and pioneer women were bringing up children they didn't have the time or resources to do any more than cover the basics: shelter, food and clothing. Children, to a large degree, took care of themselves, with older siblings running the younger ones while mother and father worked in the house and on the land.

By the beginning of the twentieth century, people were taking a more scientific approach to child-rearing. Intense interest in children's medical well-being heralded many childcare advancements, including baby formula in the 1930s, an innovation that saved many a young life—my mother-in-law's among them. Babies were left swaddled in prams to bathe in the fresh air, and also to cry on their own. American paediatrician Dr Luther Emmett Holt's 'cry it out' method had become popular, following the publication in 1894 of his book *The Care and Feeding of Children*—a title I adore because it makes it sound as if every mother is a keeper at a really specialised zoo. In 1928, Dr John B Watson's book *Psychological Care of Infant and Child* admonished parents thus:

Never, never kiss your child. Never hold it in your lap. Never rock its carriage.

The comparatively gushy Dr Benjamin Spock was a revelation when his trailblazing book *The Common Sense Book of Baby and Child Care* was published in 1946. His message to parents was that they knew more about child-rearing than they thought they did, and that their instincts to pick up their children, feed them, and play with them when they felt so inclined were usually right. His book, often referred to as *Baby and Child Care*, is still on the market. Dog-eared copies were passed around neighbourhoods in the 1950s, and babies were, once again, kissed and cuddled without concern. It was also after World War II that women more and more began to struggle with their desire to work outside the home while also rearing children, according to Dr Jan Pryor, former Chief Families Commissioner. In her 2005 address 'Children in Changing Family Structures' she said:

> Women were increasingly highly educated, but not able to use their education once married. The wave of feminism in the second half of the twentieth century gave impetus to women to go back into the workforce by choice, rather than necessity.

In the 1960s and 1970s attachment parenting was the norm and mothers were expected to instantly meet their children's needs and wants. Developed by psychologist John Bowlby, attachment theory was based on observations of children separated from their parents during World War II, either as European refugees or Londoners sent into the countryside to escape air raids. Bowlby surmised that close psychological and physical attachment was vital for promoting a sense of security in small children. But it had its drawbacks too. 'Mothers were now responsible for the physical, emotional, psychological and intellectual development of their children and were held responsible for any apparent inadequacies or abnormalities,' wrote Jane Harrison of the University of Canterbury in her 2003 doctoral thesis on motherhood identity in New Zealand. Attachment parenting was 'time-consuming, emotionally demanding and financially expensive', she concluded.

The expectation that women would sacrifice their own needs for those of their children—while still widely held, and arguably more punitive than it's ever been—was considered problematic by the end of the 1960s, says Harrison. Psychiatrist Dr Fraser McDonald coined the term 'suburban neurosis' to describe what happened when women's idealistic expectations of marriage and family life were not met. There was an increase in women abusing drugs, experiencing psychiatric problems and attempting suicide. The 'happy housewife' image was in tatters and contemporary publications such as *Thursday* magazine chronicled this shift.

These days, mothering is widely treated as a profession, especially by career women who are used to setting targets, meeting deadlines and exceeding performance expectations so they can collect bonuses or promotions. We are accustomed to seeking expert help for everything from an eyebrow groom to a lawn trim—our baby's colic and seeming disinterest in educational puzzles is no different. Of modern mothering, Jane Harrison says:

> The specific skills required to foster the healthy physical, emotional and cognitive development of a child must be acquired with the help of professionals.

Thus the good mother is believed to be 'active and interventionist'.

Mothers who take a more laissez-faire approach are often mocked and criticised. This is usually masked in a layer of concern: 'Do you think your son might like a haircut?' or 'Wouldn't little Rosie rather run around outside than watch *In the Night Garden*?' or 'Is that enough milk for a growing boy?'

In their book *The Mommy Myth: The Idealization of Motherhood and How It Has Undermined All Women*, Americans Susan J Douglas and Meredith W Michaels decry 'the new momism', a term they created to describe the guilt mothers experience when led to believe that the choices they make for their child—food, school, activities—are somehow disadvantaging them. Perhaps the most insidious aspect of the new momism is the trend towards 'intensive mothering'. They write:

Intensive mothering insists that mothers acquire professional-level skills such as those of therapist, paediatrician, consumer-products safety-inspector, and teacher, and that they lavish every ounce of physical vitality they have, the monetary equivalent of the gross domestic product of Australia, and most of all, every single bit of their emotional, mental, and psychic energy on their kids.

Not only does this place children at the top of the family hierarchy, where they arguably do not belong and would rather not sit, it places mothers at the bottom, serving everyone's needs but their own—because, after all, a 'good mother' is one who looks after everyone else first. And then there is the competitive nature of intensive mothering, which Douglas and Michaels deem 'the ultimate female Olympics':

> We are all in powerful competition with each other, in constant danger of being trumped by the mom down the street, or in the magazine that we're reading. The competition isn't just over who's a good mother—it's over who's the best.

Unfortunately, a lot of us believe that there is one best way to parent, which cannot possibly be true given the diversity of families and children. Carl Honoré, a writer who advises against micro-managing children, said in a *Time* magazine article titled 'The Growing Backlash Against Overparenting' by Nancy Gibbs:

> People feel there's somehow a secret formula for parenting, and if we just read enough books and spend enough money and drive ourselves hard enough, we'll find it and all will be okay. Can you think of anything more sinister?

You may like to point out to any hot-housing parents you know that the best toy for a toddler, according to developmental molecular biologist John Medina, author of *Brain Rules for Baby*, is a cardboard box, some fresh crayons and two hours. Language DVDs for littlies don't work, he says. Playing Mozart to the baby in utero doesn't make it any smarter, he says. Educational toys are a waste of money, he says. And people are listening—he is a *New York Times* bestselling author and go-to man for commentary on children's brains.

The counter movement is upon us, and thank heavens for that. Feminist writer Erica Jong penned an explosive *Wall Street Journal* article on modern mothering titled 'Mother Madness'. She took a stand against the past two decades of what she terms 'motherphilia', in which mothering has been glorified and commodified to the degree that a baby is seen in some quarters as the ultimate fashion accessory and a status symbol. Of course, once they have a child, these fashionable mummies realise the true impact of their decision:

> Women feel not only that they must they be everpresent for their children, but also that they must breastfeed, make their own baby food and eschew disposable diapers. It's a prison for mothers and . . . a backlash against women's freedom.

She also points out that once a woman has given up her previous life for her child she is rewarded by that child's natural and healthy detachment from her as he grows. It's a real issue, because she will still have decades to fill with some productive work—paid or unpaid—and may have no idea of what that might be.

The thing about mothering trends is that whichever philosophy is currently in vogue is held to be 'the truth' about what is best for children. It used to be 'true' that babies were manipulative little creatures who cried to mess with our heads and should be left to 'cry it out'. It used to be 'true' that only by wearing your baby on your body like a scarf could you provide her with the comfort and reassurance she required. Today in Australasia we aim for a combination of 'cry it out' and attachment parenting, with a side dish of professionalisation, so that mothers treat their role as a job to be performed to an agreed set of specifications that provide a marker of their social status. In addition, there is an unspoken social contract concerning appropriate mothering conversations. You can chit-chat about spit-up and teething problems, but you can't talk about your despair at leaving your job or your fear of having a second child when you don't feel you are managing the first all that well. There are some baby topics that are taboo.

This too will change, and in the meantime perhaps we'd be best served to figure out what works for us, our children and our circumstances so that we can live our most fulfilled and happy lives. We have generations of experience to draw from, a roll-call of sisters-in-arms whose lives we can learn lessons from. We are, as a group, better educated, more widely travelled and more globally aware than any women before us. Which means that ultimately we have no-one to blame but ourselves.

Even so, Dita, mother of two, feels there needs to be more discussion about choice:

On a fundamental level I think the option of doing something other than having kids is never put before women, so although I believe I would have always had children, I also think that it is important to be told that, actually, there are alternatives.

Gillian, mother of two, simply asks for understanding:

It starts in pregnancy. We now know that folic acid prevents spina bifida, which parents of my mother's generation did not. On the other hand, being told to eat right in pregnancy or your child will be obese is just depressing, especially when the only thing you don't throw up is a cheese and chutney sandwich.

In the enormous swag bag of difficult adjustments that come with reproducing, one of the most baffling to get to grips with is your sudden change in status. You walk into hospital a fully formed woman, with a history, some bad habits, a few embarrassing stories, a lifetime's hard-won sense of self and you walk out a . . . mother. And to most people (including, most critically, the little bundle you have dressed in some carefully chosen pastel going-home outfit) that is all you are and will be for some time to come: a mother. This is both amazing and wonderful. It is also annoying and reductive and really, really hard to get used to. Because you were, and still are, obviously—unless you signed up for the complimentary lobotomy-with-birth plan—a whole lot more besides.

A lot of women struggle to hold onto their sense of self when they have a child:

* Can they still be a bit edgy?
* Must they now take an interest in consumer reports comparing prams?
* Do they have to give up skinny dipping and vaguely dangerous pursuits like horse riding, river rafting and discount shopping?

When she had children, Lisa, mother of two, felt like the invisible woman. No-one noticed the amount of work she was putting into her children, no-one praised her job performance. She was just there in the background, getting on with things, and feeling a teeny bit resentful:

> I felt like I wasn't that important anymore, after always having to put babies first. I also found it hard because I wasn't achieving anything tangible like I was when I was working. You can't really see any progress, and people don't tell you often enough that you are doing a good job.

A lot of new mothers feel unappreciated and spend a surprising amount of time trying to jolly themselves out of it: 'I'm so lucky my child is healthy! I'm so lucky my partner changes nappies!' they tell themselves. Of course, you're not supposed to admit to anyone that you are anything less than ecstatic about all facets of your new life with your new baby. As Caroline, mother of two, explains:

I wish more mothers talked about how shit it all gets! It's normal to cry for no reason, to dread picking up your baby, to curl your toes at the thought of breast-feeding. Knowing more mums were going through this would take away a lot of the sense of failure that overwhelms in the first few months.

When I brought my baby home I thought that I should be Miss Manners. I would never swear in front of him, or say anything mean about anyone else within earshot, including politicians and sports stars, I would never smack the dog's nose in front of the baby, or bite my nails on the sofa while he played next to me on the floor. All my yucky habits and lesser traits would be expunged! Except I am human, so that didn't happen.

My hunch is that you will experience something similar.

At three hours past nap-time, when your toddler is stumbling drunkenly round the lounge, bouncing off the coffee table, tripping over mega-blocks, and you pop a calming dummy into his mouth that he shoots straight back out again like a carnival attraction and shakes his head—'No!'—you may find yourself saying something like this: 'Either we do this, or we don't do this. Mummy doesn't give a shit any more.'

You won't be proud of yourself and you might not be able to laugh at yourself for some days, but you should because it is these unexpected moments that will come to dominate your life. Don't worry, though, you will soon learn how to deal with them. This is when you back away from the child, straighten your shoulders, take a deep breath and march straight into the kitchen, toddler glued to you like a discarded piece of chewing gum, and put the kettle on. A sixth coffee today won't do too much harm, will it?

Or you might be driving between the supermarket, home and mall, that grim mummy triumvirate, your impressionable precious cargo throwing toys around the back seat and yelling 'yum-yum' because he is hungry and you forgot to pack a snack, and some sweetheart in a black SUV cuts you off. You might say, 'Excuse me, asshole!' and then wonder how long it will be until your little dude, now familiar with 'no', 'up', 'more', will add 'asshole' to his repertoire, and choose to use it publicly for the first time when he is round at your mother-in-law's house.

I could call these hypothetical examples but I am afraid that would be lying, and there's enough of that going around already. The good news is that, with time, you will learn to cope with these sticky situations far more elegantly, and they will come to form the basis of some of your favourite mothering stories—to be shared only with your closest and most trusted confidantes, of course.

Some women, when they become mothers, seem to undergo a personality transplant. Suddenly the woman you knew, the one who liked to wear slightly whoreish studded leather stilettos and go to foreign film festivals is gone, replaced by a woman who wears an abundance of pink and will happily listen to the Wiggles on repeat in the car. Viewing this charitably you would have to assume that the weight of responsibility in nurturing a little one has pushed them toward stereotypical, socially acceptable mummy behaviour. It can be really difficult to fashion a mummy identity that suits you, especially if you never felt particularly maternal before falling pregnant, if you didn't expect you would ever have children, or if some of those typical mummy traits don't attract you. And then you have the various mummy varieties—yummy mummy, slummy mummy, eco-mummy, alpha mummy—cooked up by creative news writers and foisted upon you, which do have some basis in reality but have been completely skewed for the entertainment of the masses. These identities are like the Spice Girls, cute and fun but ultimately not real, and should also be consigned to the last millennium.

Being presented with these options when you are formulating your new lifestyle is incredibly unhelpful. They are not to be bought into—not for a second—but in the belief that knowledge is power and snark is good for the soul, here is a brief rundown on the mummy types other people may try to attribute to your good and blameless self.

Yummy mummy: She is the sexy one, the mummy who returns to her pre-baby form quickly and with little fuss, and continues to attract male attention in the way a dewy tropical flower attracts hummingbirds. She is universally loathed/ envied/feared by other mothers, not least because her child is a chubby-cheeked accessory that serves to make her look more sylphlike and desirable.

Slummy mummy: She is the lazy one who bollockses everything up. She arrives at the school gate in saggy tracky-daks and food-stained Ugg boots, never manages to drop the final five kilos, and is most likely to buy supermarket cupcakes and pass them off as her own work. She is possibly the most popular mummy type in British media today. (Brits have a particular fascination for the mummy varieties, possibly because there are so many wonderfully bitchy British journalists who write about cultural phenomena.)

Alpha mummy: She is the working mum, and legend has it she will focus as much energy and determination into producing perfect children as she does to achieve her work–life goals. She is always pushed for time, always striving for more, and she's always a bit pale and anxious looking. In news articles she is often represented by a twiggy young model in a business suit holding a briefcase in one hand and a baby bottle in the other.

Eco-mummy: Possessing a laudable concern for the environment—but in a really beautiful *Dwell* magazine sort of way—eco-mummy is queen of the organic market. She also has a garden to die for, a groovy vintage wardrobe and an amazing collection of rare crockery. Her home is cool and original and she is never more than twenty minutes away from a bang-up dinner cooked from scratch. She is a souped-up Felicity Kendall from *The Good Life*.

Professional mummy, aka prommie: She is the Type-A stay-at-home mummy who does everything brilliantly. In a former life she was a lawyer or research chemist, but now she funnels all her ambition into her hapless offspring, who almost always have retro-chic Edwardian names and designer wardrobes. The prommie is responsible for the escalating birthday-party problem—she was the first to hire a bouncy castle, clown and Shetland pony for her child's third birthday party and now everyone else feels obligated to at least get a kick-ass cake made.

Helicopter mum: A recent addition, she is the uptight control freak who is always close at hand and wants to be involved in all aspects of her children's lives—long after it's appropriate. She will turn up in class to drop off homework (that she has done herself), invite herself on every school camp, and bully her 23-year-old son's boss when an expected promotion goes to someone else.

Free-range mum: At the opposite end of the parental supervision spectrum, she is, nonetheless, anxious in her own way. She is concerned that her children learn independence and survival skills which will advantage them in later life. Her philosophy is based on pleasant memories of walking alone to school as a child and being let out of the house at weekends and told to 'return before sundown'. One of the most infamous free-range mums is New Yorker Lenore Skenazy, who dropped off her nine-year-old son in the handbag department at Bloomingdales department store armed with a map, travel-card and $20 and told him to find his own way home. She garnered so much attention for this stunt that she started a blog which has since turned into a book. In hysterical fashion, the US media dubbed her 'America's worst mom'.

Now you know what these so-called representative mummy types are about, you are free to ignore them at your leisure.

There is a widespread belief that while mothering is challenging—especially for those women who combine it with a working life—it is a juggling act that is, ultimately, personally rewarding and of benefit to society as a whole, given that mothers raise our future leaders, employers, artists, builders, plumbers and doctors. Birthing and raising children is considered important work (although not work that needs to be compensated or even formally recognised as really freaking hard). Interviews with New Zealand mothers revealed that they believed that even if they were struggling with motherhood, other women were not struggling. The choices that women have today to design a lifestyle of work, childcare, partnership and leisure are generally seen as a positive. Dita, mother of two, says:

> I absolutely do not think mothering is harder than in times past, and if it is, it's only because we have chosen bigger goals for ourselves. For me to claim that I have it harder than my Italian grandmother, who had ten children in post-war Italy, or my Kiwi grandmother, who milked cows every day while raising four children, or even my own mother, with her various struggles, would be ludicrous. I have choice. If I have a big

mortgage to pay off or a career to uphold while raising children, those are things I choose and I can't expect too much sympathy for them, I don't think.

Melissa, mother of two, tries to keep things in perspective:

The challenge around being a mother at this point in time are all around what is in our heads—what we are supposed to act like, look like, what activities our children 'need' to go to, how much time we are supposed to give them, etcetera. I have actively tried to take out the word 'should' when it comes to parenting as it only makes me feel bad and I do know that I am doing the best I can right now and it is good enough.

In the United States, parenting is widely perceived as much harder than it was in decades past. In a survey conducted in 2007, Pew Research found that 70 per cent of Americans believe parenthood is more challenging than it was in the 1970s and 1980s, when most of today's parents were growing up, and they think the current generation of parents is doing a worse job.

I would argue that we are experiencing a shift towards that point of view on this side of the world, and with good reason. While no-one wants to revisit the days of washing clothing by hand, cooking over an open fire, or losing multiple offspring to childhood diseases, many mothers feel that they have a tougher time of it than their forebears—mostly because they think they have to live up to some ideal mother. The fact that this woman does not—and in reality could not—exist does not stop new mothers, especially, from falling victim to comparison with her, weighing their performance against this mythic creature who has laid down her life in service to her children, who crafts every morsel of food that crosses their lips, maintains a beautiful, child-friendly home, gets involved in numerous educational and developmentally friendly activities, organises magical play days and parties, eats well and looks like a catalogue model, works in some glamorous job that doesn't sap her energy or make her resent her children, and maintains a romantic and rock-solid bond with her partner.

Maree, mother of two, is emphatic:

Is it harder to be a mother today? *Yes!* Why do we all have to think we can be superwoman? Babies, perfectly manicured homes and gardens, careers. I hate the fact that as modern women we feel guilty taking 'time out' to raise our children.

Deborah, mother of two, says:

It's harder in some ways—despite dishwashers and other labour-saving devices—because everyone is so obsessive and angsty about it. But in my view they are obsessive and angsty about the wrong things, and scarily are often using their children to meet their own emotional needs, which is very destructive. Parents should be there to meet the child's emotional needs, not vice versa.

Sophie, mother of one, agrees that standards have never been higher:

The expectation now is to work, provide, be a role model, a mentor, and to do everything 100 per cent. Those expectations weren't there when I was a child and my mother had four children. I do think there is a conscious thing of being a supermum and doing everything yourself.

Jackie, mother of two boys, says:

I guess it's easy to say it's harder for us than in previous generations, but I think it actually is. I think the way women are portrayed on TV and in magazines is a major contributor—Angelina Jolie is a classic example. Look at her—she's an actress, got a gorgeous husband, fifteen kids, wants to save the world and still looks fabulous every day!

Despite your best intentions and firm attempts to avoid buying into this crap, you will probably at some point fall victim to the awesome power of the 'supermum', the Loch Ness monster of mothering. Emerging from the mists in the 1980s around the same time that Michael Keaton made a lame joke of stay-at-home fathers in the film *Mr Mom*, the supermum is a fearful creature, the woman who does everything—paid work, tend children, cook, bake, keep house, exercise, maintain friendships, manage finances—to a very high standard. She has everything we supposedly all want.

British writer India Knight says the supermum is actually just a woman of means, who can afford to pay people to bake biscuits for the school fete while she works at her high-powered job in the financial district. In a column for the *Sunday Times* called 'A working mother's first job is to be our scapegoat', she wrote:

You might as well call every aristocratic parent going back 300 years a supermum—ooh, look she's wearing couture and hosting a ball, even though she has children and 200 deer; I wonder how she does it. I mean, really.

You might think the easiest way to vanquish this monster is to stop behaving as if she could ever exist and to get on with your imperfect, bumbling life in which you leave the house in wrinkled clothing, eat too many processed foods and, occasionally, allow your baby to watch Elmo. Sounds good, but it can be hard to stick to this pledge when you are surrounded by women who try to be supermum and to lag behind them is to imply you don't want to be the best mother you can be. This is when the lying kicks into overdrive. 'Of course, I feed him puréed spinach every night. I would never let my child subsist for days on custard and kransky sausages. Never.'

'Yesterday, a mum pointed out that my son had an alarming red spot on the back of his scalp,' said Kaila, mother of three, who is refreshingly honest about her perceived foibles.

'I blandly explained that it was just where his sister had dribbled powdered chalk on his head. I did not elaborate on how many days it had been there or that they were grinding chalk in an effort to amuse themselves since I had neglected to arrange an after-school activity for half the days of the week. *Shame on me!'*

There are a lot of supermum-wannabes out there, power-walking behind fancy prams on their way to coffee group, where they will persecute the less able. (I exaggerate, but not much.) They would lead you to believe explicitly—by telling you about their wonderful routines with their wonderful babies—or implicitly through their own manifest capability, that mothering for them is just not that hard. In my experience, the stay-at-home supermum-wannabes are most formidable. Having made the choice to pour all their time and ambition into their kids, they are not generally troubled by the sense that there is anything more they could do, which is a very powerful position to be in and unfortunately can lead to smugness.

They do not beat themselves up over Soviet-style regimented daycare for babies or worry about their children coming home from school to an empty pantry. And in some cases this sureness leaves them the mental space to pass judgment on the other mums, the ones with the dirty ponytails and tired, drool-soaked babies. Mostly, though, the stay-at-home supermum-wannabes simply put vast amounts of pressure on themselves to perform flawlessly and their apparent perfection is what makes the other mothers feel crap.

'I say we leave the supermums on their end of the

playground and assemble under our own banner, 'REAL MUMS, UNITE!,' says Kaila. 'Hopefully they can read it through the spilled coffee on the bottom left corner.'

For all us ordinary mums—and I believe that's 99 per cent of us—columns like India Knight's are reassuring at a life stage when we need all the reassurance we can get. Pragmatic psychologist Nigel Latta, author of *Before Your Kids Drive You Crazy Read This!: Battlefield Wisdom for Stressed Out Parents* and a crop of other popular parenting books, is similarly soothing. Basically he tells us that we know what we're doing and the kids will turn out all right. Stop over-thinking every parental choice, stop treating the kids like mini adults, stop freaking out. *Above all, stop freaking out.*

We only need professionals like Latta to tell us we're okay because we don't have enough people in our day-to-day lives telling us that we're okay. Part of this is due to the loss of community over the last fifty or so years. Modern families are more isolated than they used to be for a variety of reasons, including urbanisation, the increased number of women in the workplace, fear of strangers, financial pressures and the fact that we seek entertainment in our homes—television, DVDs, Wii, computers, Xbox, swimming pools, tennis courts, games rooms—rather than going out. We are less likely to join work-related organisations, to be part of clubs, to go to church or volunteer to help others. This lack of participation erodes what Harvard University academic Robert D Putnam, author of *Bowling Alone: The Collapse and Revival of American Community*, calls our 'social capital', which is the bonds between people that make a community work. We are increasingly disconnected from family, friends and neighbours, and it's rending our social fabric.

As Sarah, mother of two, says:

Women used to talk over the fence. They had each other. They would've had problems for sure, but they were only a cup of sugar or a gin and tonic away from a sounding board, or company. The 'company' thing is so important. I don't think our mothers and grandmothers were afflicted to the same degree with the idea of being perfect—doing it all right. They had different pressures, but it certainly seems as though it were simpler.

There is also a perception that children have it harder now, too, that their lives are more complicated and endangered than in decades past. As Jackie explains:

There are so many more pressures being put upon our children these days, which makes parenting a nightmare. Cyberbullying, drugs, and the huge array of material possessions kids try to outdo each other with, are all things that previous generations didn't have to worry about. My mother didn't have to worry about P, text bullying, Facebook or the internet when she was raising me. I think protecting our kids these days is a lot harder but at the same time you can't wrap them up in cotton wool 24/7. We just have to try and be sensible and keep doing the best we can.

Jo, a mother of one and a secondary school teacher, concurs:

Now that my daughter is thirteen, I think there are a huge number of pressures that weren't there in the past. Attitudes—respect, answering back, the way you talk to people, interacting—are different, technology and peer pressure are massive factors, there are so many more layers to negotiate. I see this every day in the choices my students are expected to make. Children now expect to have a 'say' in everything and sometimes it is very difficult to just say 'I am the adult and my decision stands'. It is very different. It is a complex and difficult job these days.

Erica Jong theorises in the *Wall Street Journal* that the obsessive drive for mothering perfection, as personified by the supermum, is seated in our fears about the world that we live in—the sense that despite lower crime and accident rates, children are more at risk than they've ever been:

What is so troubling about these theories of parenting—both pre- and postnatal—is that they seem like attempts to exert control in a world that is increasingly out of control. We can't get rid of the carcinogens in the environment, but we can make sure that our kids arrive at school each day with a reusable lunch bag full of produce from the farmers' market. We can't do anything about loose nukes falling into the hands of terrorists, but we can make sure that our progeny's every waking hour is tightly scheduled with edifying activities.

According to Patricia Somers from the University of Texas, in this age of smaller families, parents feel compelled to guard their offspring more jealously simply because they don't have as many chances to usher a child successfully into adulthood to become a reproductive unit. To preserve our own genetic material, we have to throw all our attention and worry at the comparatively fewer children we do have. Hovering helicopter parents are not a middle-class phenomenon, she argues, but exist in all strata of society.

Julie, mother of two, explains:

Parents are so concerned about boosting kids' self-esteem so it's 'healthy', I think they go overboard and often make kids too full of themselves and arrogant. Which then makes them harder to parent: cheekier, bolshy, and badly behaved as they get older.

Fiona, mother of two, talks about the loss of community:

I do think that a Western lifestyle makes parenting difficult in that we tend to live in a society that is based on the nuclear family rather than on a local community, so there is often less availability of hands-on support for mums and babies. My stepdaughter's partner is Fijian and has told me that in traditional Fijian culture a baby spends the first week of its life in a relative's arms, not being set down at all.

It would be fair to say that mothers in New Zealand's cities—especially Auckland, Wellington and Christchurch—lug an extra basket of 'concerns', tied to status and money. In rural areas, there is not the same intensity in the drive to make children 'successful' in an easily recognisable way—through attendance at a private school, international class trips, and expensive after-school activities, such as rock-climbing and scuba diving. That's not to say there aren't pockets of hot-house parenting and angst in Warkworth, Taihape and Westport because they're everywhere, but chances are greater that you will find yourself in conversation with a parent who makes you feel inadequate over the brand of your baby's car seat in Remuera than in Levin.

Andrea, a mother of two in Auckland's wealthy eastern suburbs, often feels that her children are not as privileged as their classmates, and while she doesn't think they are missing out on anything, she would like to be able to provide more. She and her husband moved house so their children could attend better schools, but this has brought them into a circle of families with more assets and more luxurious lifestyles. She explains:

The problem of which school to attend wasn't so much an issue decades ago, whereas it's really big now. Plus more women work full time so are more tired in the after-noons and evenings and find the demands of parenting harder while still trying to be it all—good mother, good wife, maintain the figure, hobbies and friends.

Competitiveness kicks in early, with parents putting their young children on waiting lists for 'the best' preschools before they even turn one, hunting out the most successful baby swim school, and swapping notes on childcare that emphasises developmental activities that might advantage littlies when they get to school. For example, Micah was on the waiting list for his Mainly Music group for a year because its reputation is such that families clamour from all over the area to shake their tambourines there.

Kylie, who balances work with raising two daughters, says that while babyhood was challenging for its relentlessness, parenting school-aged children is about being a Jill-of-all-trades:

> Now it's more about being a massive expert in all fields—a listener, a friend, a cook, a taxi driver, a motivator, a playmate, a doctor, etcetera.

She feels driven to try to excel in all these arenas (some of which generally require university degrees and long apprenticeships) while also being an exemplary employee, supportive friend, and partner to her husband.

Julie, mother of two, says:

> My mum thinks parents [of her generation] didn't consider everything the way we do—and tie themselves in

knots, worrying—to provide the absolute best for our kids, which is stressful. There are more temptations for a sedentary lifestyle with so much TV, Xbox and computers that we have to fight, whereas years ago kids just went outside to play without being pushed. Kids can't just roam after school like they used to, or get themselves to clubs, they have to be taken to activities. They also have to be supervised more closely.

But Joanna, with two children and a demanding part-time job, believes modern mothers are much better off, even with their frantic lives:

I think nearly everything is better now—less physical housework, more opportunities to define yourself, perhaps a fuller but more frantic life. The downside is that our families are more scattered so there is less support. A huge advance is that fathers are much more involved these days and express love verbally and physically more than previous generations.

Maria, mother of two, says:

There is the theory that it was emotionally easier [to be a mother in decades past] because you didn't have so many choices, so much pressure to send your child to preschool Italian class or Baby Pilates, or whatever is on offer these days. But I don't know. I think the key is the support you have around you. I found it terribly hard because I came to New Zealand from England and knew no one, was working full-time and had to pay students to be with the kids. I remember asking my mum, 'Didn't you find it hard getting around without a car?'. She looked surprised and said 'No, I left you with Auntie Doris when I needed to shop'. Doris was in fact a neighbour but very close, like a blood relative. Without some kind of support network I think motherhood is the hardest job in the world.

And that probably sums up our biggest challenge as mothers in this new century: we try to do everything ourselves, feeling somehow that asking for help is failure, that the success or not of our child rests entirely on our shoulders. It seems our hard-won independence is making it harder for us to parent.

Further reading

Contemporary Motherhood: The Impact of Children on Adult Time by Lyn Craig, Ashgate Publishing, 2007

The Mommy Myth: The Idealization of Motherhood and How It Has Undermined All Women by Susan J Douglas and Meredith W Michaels, Free Press, 2004

'Mother Madness' by Erica Jong, *Wall Street Journal*, 6 November 2010

'I love you more' by Susan Dominus, *New York Times*, 10 May 2009

'A Working Mother's First Job Is to Be Our Scapegoat' by India Knight, *The Times*, 10 August 2008

'The Traitor and the Hedonist: The Mythology of Motherhood in Two New Zealand Child Abuse Cases' by Dr Linda Jean Kenix, University of Canterbury, presented at the international meeting of the International Communication Association, TBA, Montreal, Canada, 21 May 2008

'UNICEF, The Childcare Transition, Innocenti Report Card 8', The United Nations Children's Fund, 2008

'Relax and Enjoy Kids', by Nigel Latta, *New Zealand Herald*, 3 June 2007

'How Serfdom Saved the Women's Movement: Dispatches from the Nanny Wars' by Caitlin Flanagan, *Atlantic*, March 2004

Lenore Skenazy at freerangekids.wordpress.com

'The Kiwi Nest: 60 Years of Change in New Zealand Families', Families Commission, 1 June 2008 at familiescommission. govt.nz/research/the-kiwi-nest

9. The hot-button topics

Wonderful, something else to argue about

Silly girl. You thought your decision to have a baby and all the subsequent decisions regarding that baby's welfare were yours to make, and yours alone. Not a chance. Besides the obvious stakeholders—your baby's father, extended family, other caregivers—you will be expected to defend your choices to all comers at morning teas, outings at the park, book club meetings and Playcentre Christmas parties. While 'naff off' is nearly always a reasonable response to 'helpful' people who want to know why you have decided to do things the way you have, sometimes it is handy (and more satisfying) to have some stock answers ready.

As much as you'd like to believe you can continue in the same vein as you have conducted the rest of your adult life, suiting yourself and taking into due consideration those factors that you deem relevant, and ignoring everything else, you can't. You will be unexpectedly and unwillingly thrust into impromptu debates with the intensity, if not the import, of UN Global Forum meetings. Given that you will more than likely be tired and distracted when this happens, I have prepared a series of cheat sheets for such circumstances.

Home birth vs hospital birth

* It is not known exactly how many women give birth at home in New Zealand each year, but Home Birth Aotearoa, the national body representing home birth associations throughout the country, estimates the number to be seven per cent of total births, or around 2200 a year. In some parts of the country—the West Coast is offered as an example—home births are said to make up ten per cent of the total. New Zealand's rate is well above that of Australia and the United States, where it is estimated home births make up less than one per cent of total births each year, and the United Kingdom, with a home birth rate of around three per cent. The developed country with the highest home birth rate is the Netherlands, at around 30 per cent.

* The philosophy behind home birthing is thus: because pregnancy is not an illness, giving birth following a non-risk pregnancy does not require hospitalisation. Proponents say women feel most comfortable in their own home where they can control the setting, from ambient lighting to music and the number of people attending the birth. This, they say, can foster a less stressful and even less painful birth. Because you are at home, pain relief is limited to non-medical measures including breathing

exercises, aromatherapy, massage and different labour positions. If you decide part-way through your labour that the pain is too much for you, it is usually too late to do anything about it, so you have to be confident about your feelings on this from the outset.

* Of course, the major sticking point with home birth—and it is significant—is that if anything goes wrong, you are not in a hospital setting, where emergency equipment and medical professionals are available to help you and your baby. That means you need to have great faith in your midwife, who will make the call if you need to transfer to hospital due to a complication in labour. There have been multiple high-profile instances around the world where midwives have made the call too late and babies' lives have been lost. Babies also die at hospital, of course, but if there are complications you have a better chance in a hospital. Given my past miscarriage, my age and my positive feelings about the work done in hospitals, I wouldn't have done it any other way, but I support choice in maternal care and think women who want to give birth at home have every right to do so.

* There are not many midwives who are prepared to oversee home births (and even fewer doctors); a list is available from Home Birth Aotearoa. Those that do say they feel privileged to be invited into women's homes to help them celebrate a new life. Jane, mother of two, gave birth at home twice following a traumatic stillbirth at five months which gave her bad associations with the hospital. She says: 'There was no way I was going to go back into

hospital to deliver another baby, so I chose home birth. It was fantastic for me to build up my well-being and confidence in myself and my body.'

* In the end, this is an intensely personal choice, and a highly emotional one. Home births sometimes go wrong. Hospital births sometimes go wrong, too. You must inform yourself, search your heart and choose the path that feels right for you.

Toughing it out vs epidural

* Epidurals are fast becoming the norm in certain sectors of New Zealand with an estimated 30 per cent of women electing to use the powerful pain relief during childbirth. Women aged in their 30s and Asian and European women are most likely to choose an epidural, a form of localised anaesthetic which numbs your lower body, according to the Ministry of Health's 'Report on Maternity'. In Australia the rate is also around 30 per cent, while in the United Kingdom it is approaching 40 per cent and in the United States is 60 per cent.

* Hospitals and doctors' practices run workshops on epidurals, so you can get a handle on the risks and benefits when you still have time to consider alternatives. Having been to one, I would say these workshops can raise more fears than they allay, with couples stumbling on technical information and writing copious notes that may not make a lot of sense when they re-read them later. At my doctor's epidural workshop there were even drinks and nibbles, a

friendly attempt to make it seem like the fun, social occasion it most definitely was not.

* One of the arguments against the use of epidurals to assist birth is that they can lead to further interventions, but many women don't realise this is the case and they unwittingly end up having a highly medicalised birthing experience. Epidurals leave a woman temporarily paralysed from the waist down, unable to leave the bed until the drug has worn off. They can slow down labour, necessitating the use of the drug pitocin (a synthetic form of the hormone oxytocin, which stimulates contractions) to speed things up and this may sometimes lead to an emergency caesarian to get the baby out.

* Like any medical procedure, there are risks. This is a serious jab delivered a hair's breadth away from your precious, vulnerable spinal cord. Possible complications include severe headache, lower back pain after labour (which can persist for some months), lasting numbness, shivering and itchy skin. For babies it can cause irritability and interfere with the sucking reflex, making that first attempt at nursing problematic.

* Because you can't feel what's happening in your nethers, you will need a catheter to allow you to urinate, a point that had escaped me until it came time for the doctor to insert one. I thought this would be horrible, but it really was no big deal. I also ended up in stirrups, which had been my ultimate birthing nightmare before I got to hospital; it seemed so old-school, like giving birth in an experimental 1960s film with a soundtrack by Deep Purple. Again,

it was no biggie. The main thing was to get the baby born safely, and we did.

* If you choose to have a natural birth, there are other forms of pain relief available to you. Spa baths are effective for some women, as is acupressure and the TENS (transcutaneous electrical nerve stimulation) machine, which tricks the brain into focusing on the localised tingling it produces rather than the labour pains. Music, visualisation and aromatherapy are all considered helpful.

There is something heroic about giving birth the old-fashioned way—the way, in truth, that most women around the world still do it. I remember my third-form science teacher standing up at the front of the lab in her white coat and brown lace-ups, telling us how amazing it was to give birth with no drugs, how she concentrated on her husband's encouragement, not the labour, and how she had forgotten the pain moments after it was over anyway. 'You don't think about it, because you have this wonderful baby in your arms!' she crowed. I think this was around the same time that the lady from Tampax came to the lab to give us hot pink tampon holders and teach us about the monthly cycle, so it was a relevant if slightly ugh-inducing story. (Our science teacher *has sex*? Eeuw!)

At the time I thought my teacher was mad, but twenty years later, as a pregnant woman considering just how natural I wanted my son's birth to be, and muddled by the stories I heard from friends and antenatal class, I was convinced that she had been made of sterner stuff than I—that when it came time to push I just didn't have what it took to do it without help.

My birth plan took a bob each way, saying that I would aim for a drug-free birth, but would take advice on the day. I had only filled out a birth plan because I had to, not because I actually intended to follow it step by step—I was convinced that events would take on a life of their own. I had been warned by friends not to become wedded to the birth plan because theirs had gone out the window when they had emergency caesarian sections.

As it turned out, my doctor made the decision for me following more than twelve hours of unproductive labour, and having an epidural was the right choice. Without one I may not have had enough strength left to push; there was a good chance I would have been forced to undergo a caesarian, which I *really* did not want. Having gone the epidural route once, I would be more inclined to do it again—I have to be honest. None of my fears transpired, and it was calming for both me and my exhausted husband, who was able to take a nap while we waited for the cervix to dilate.

Caesarian vs vaginal birth

* There is a misconception that women who do not want to go through the pain of childbirth or prefer the convenience of scheduling their birth are driving a growing trend towards caesarian sections. Not true. In her PhD thesis: 'Caesarian Birth: Too Posh to Push, or Punished for not Pushing? Exploring Women's Experiences of Caesarian Birth', Leanne Taylor-Miller of the University of

Auckland found that few mothers actually requested a caesarian and that even planned caesarians are often not the choice of the mothers, but a medical necessity advised by a doctor.

* About a quarter of births in New Zealand are via caesarian section (and rising) but the overwhelming preference societally is for traditional vaginal births that are considered better for babies and mothers, and more authentic to boot. After all, a caesarian section is major surgery and it can interfere with the bonding between a mother and baby. It's no hay-ride, but stories about elective caesars tend to imply it is a paint-by-numbers procedure that slots nicely between appointments at the hairdresser and the gym. The reality is that many mothers find themselves housebound after a caesarian birth, unable to drive a car or even pick up their new baby for weeks.

* As mother-of-three Gillian says, 'If you had a caesarian like my first one where I could not stand upright for six weeks, you wouldn't tell me I took the easy option.' Mothers in this situation need support and understanding, not a lecture.

* And yet the myth prevails that women want scheduled caesarians, pester their doctors to arrange them, organise their nursery fit-out around them, then encourage all their friends that birth-by-surgery is a better experience. In our antenatal class the instructor lined up eleven or twelve people in a tiny space to approximate the cosiness of an operating theatre in which a caesarian is performed. She wanted to horrify us with the idea that a soccer team

would be part of our special family event. She was right: none of us wanted to be at the centre of that crowd having a baby. And yet it happens every day out of medical necessity and less often by choice.

Cloth nappies vs disposables

* Reports on the environmental impact of disposable nappies versus cloth nappies vary widely. Basically, dealing with baby waste is bad news for the Earth. Whether you expend power and water washing re-usable cloth nappies, or dump disposable nappies in landfills where they can take up to 500 years to degrade, the scale of the problem is considerable. The average child goes through 4000 nappies before they are toilet-trained.

* Cloth was the norm until the 1990s, when disposable nappies became widely available and their price dropped, thanks to greater competition and the Warehouse effect. Their convenience was hard to ignore.

* At the same time, the environmental debate concerning nappies kicked in. It was assumed that cloth nappies were better for the environment, despite research from manufacturers (such as Procter and Gamble) to the contrary. Recently, Allen Hershkowitz of the Natural Resources Defense Council said in a *Seattle Times* article, 'Cloth or disposables? Half-century debate still on', by Leanne Italie: 'We don't recommend one over another. A compelling argument for getting rid of disposable diapers absolutely does not exist. It's a personal choice, but it

really can't be made on environmental grounds. There are costs both ways.'

* Looking at it from a financial standpoint, cloth is your friend. Once you have outlaid for the colourful outer pants and the soft cotton inserts, it is estimated you can save between $500 and $2000 each year by using cloth.

* If you decide to use cloth nappies you can improve their eco-friendliness. The best sanitiser and whitener is free—it's sunshine. So, dry nappies on the washing line whenever possible. Using bicarbonate of soda and vinegar to clean them (as well as a pinch of detergent to deal with nasty bugs), washing them in warm rather than hot water, and handing them on to a friend when your baby has finished with them will maximise their value.

* With disposables, consider buying more expensive brands that are better-made—they won't require changing as often. Cheap nappies that fall apart within hours are a false economy and produce a bigger carbon footprint. And rather than sticking to a rigid nappy-changing schedule, you might want to consider keeping an eye on your child and changing nappies only when necessary. Eventually, your little one will tell you when they would like to be changed.

* Another factor to consider is the speed with which your child will learn to use the toilet. Anecdotal evidence suggests that babies raised in cloth nappies are quicker to get the hang of potty training because cloth nappies are less comfortable when soiled than disposables, which pull moisture away from the baby's skin.

For the record, I use disposable nappies. I wasn't willing to have dirty nappies soaking in buckets around the house, or to lumber myself with that quantity of extra washing, and we weren't in a position to pay for a nappy service. I like to think that the fact we are a one-car household and passionate train users offsets our child's nappies, but I do not kid myself that we are environmental warriors.

Immunisation vs 'natural immunity'

* The immunisation debate isn't just an intriguing example of how scientific information can be interpreted vastly differently by well-meaning people with different perspectives, it is a source of true anguish and stress for parents. No-one wants to expose their child to undue risk, or to experiment with their health, although that may not seem obvious as you read some of the emotive literature on this subject.

* When your baby is immunised, they are injected with a weakened form of the virus or bacteria responsible for the disease in question. The body's immune system is encouraged to attack the bugs and to produce protective antibodies. The effects do not last forever, which is why your child will need booster shots as they get older, and why some adults continue to get boosters for diseases such as tetanus, which can strike when you cut your finger on a rose thorn in your garden.

* Although immunisation is considered safe, there is a chance that your child will have an adverse reaction to it. Most commonly that will be a red, slightly swollen patch

of skin around the injection site, an elevated temperature and general grizzly behaviour—crying, clinginess, fatigue, loss of appetite. These effects can last for a day or two. It is very rare, but some people have an allergic reaction (anaphylaxis) to vaccines which happens very soon after injection, and is the reason you are asked to stay in the waiting room with your baby for twenty minutes after immunisation. In those cases, the doctor can administer epinephrine, or adrenaline. The chances of a significant reaction to immunisation is one or two in several million, according to the Centers for Disease Control and Prevention in the United States.

* While there is no guarantee that your child won't still contract a disease such as whooping cough or rubella the chances are vastly reduced, and children who have been immunised but still get sick tend to experience a milder form of the disease and recover more quickly, according to the Immunisation Advisory Centre based at the University of Auckland.

* Many people when weighing up their decision point to literature stating that vaccination has been linked to autism, multiple sclerosis, bowel disease and SIDS (sudden infant death syndrome) now known as SUDI (sudden unexpected death in infancy). There is no independent, verifiable research which supports these claims. The most commonly quoted piece of research is British gastroenterologist Dr Andrew Wakefield's 1998 study published in the British medical journal *The Lancet*, linking the MMR (mumps, measles, rubella) vaccine to

autism, based on tests conducted on children who had been referred to Royal Free Hospital in Hampstead for gastrointestinal complaints. However, there were several serious problems with this research and the causal argument was problematic: autism first becomes apparent in children aged around eighteen months, which happens to be just after the MMR is given—but that doesn't mean the vaccine causes autism any more than short skirts cause teenage pregnancy. In 2010, after a two-year investigation, the General Medical Council in Britain struck Dr Wakefield off the register. Months later, *The Lancet* announced they were retracting his paper from their public record.

* Some suggest there is no need to vaccinate against diseases that no longer exist in New Zealand, such as polio (poliomyelitis) and diphtheria, both of which used to be common here in the early part of the twentieth century. The problem with this reasoning is that these diseases still exist in populations overseas and are never more than a plane ride away. Some diseases, whooping cough among them, do still exist in New Zealand and can cause terrible suffering and death.

* There is also a widespread belief that it is better to allow children to build up natural immunity gradually over time rather than introduce nasty diseases to their system in the form of an injection every few months in the first years of life. Medical experts are united in the view that even very small babies can cope with immunisation. While it could be argued that the natural immunity approach works in

the case of chicken pox, which is much milder in children than adults—hence the popularity of chicken pox parties—it is simply not worth the risk against more serious diseases, such as diphtheria, which attacks the upper respiratory tract, or hepatitis B, which can cause liver disease and is believed to be the second-most common cause of cancer after smoking tobacco. UNICEF estimates that nine million lives a year are saved by immunisation, and that a further sixteen million could be saved if immunisation was wider spread.

* Finally, a word on 'herd immunity'. This is the effect of national immunisation programmes. When enough children in a population are immunised against a disease it stops circulating and even those children who have not been vaccinated are protected from its effects—epidemics do not happen. This is better for everyone living in the community. When enough people are not vaccinated, the effects of herd immunity are weakened, so the risk of an outbreak increases. For more information contact the Immunisation Advisory Centre, immune.org.nz.

Such is the concern raised by studies linking immunisation to SUDI and multiple sclerosis, that even when mothers know there is no proof that vaccination causes these conditions, they are put off. As Deborah, mother of two, says:

I haven't vaccinated my younger child. I always thought people who were iffy about vaccination were flakes but then my sister had a profoundly autistic son and it became apparent just after his MMR, so I just thought better safe than sorry, even though I know the rigorous scientific evidence says there is no link.

Sarah, a mother of twins, says:

I chose not to vaccinate when they were babies. At the time, there seemed to be a plethora of vaccinations, one for every letter of the alphabet. Later, when they turned four and before school, they were vaccinated. I see both sides, but it's a shame we can't seem to have a healthy debate without the overwhelming emotive and hostile aspect.

Gillian, mother of three, says:

I think all of the diseases are far worse than the risks of vaccination. I try to follow what I can find from research rather than the buzz with the mothers. I feel sorry for the doctors who are faced with lay people who have no professional or ethical limitations on the statements they can make.

Jane, mother of two, makes a salient point:

I have seen and worked with enough un-vaccinated kids to see the damage. I missed the six-week vaccination because I considered the babies just too tiny but did all the rest. Those who righteously claim they don't vaccinate their children depend on the likes of us to vaccinate our kids and keep their kids healthy. In my mind, that sucks.

Mother-of-two Maree, who is married to a doctor, says of her sons:

The poor little buggers have had every needle going. If you want to live all 'Victorian' be my guest. I will err on the side of modern medicine every time.

Personally, I never doubted for a moment that I would get my baby immunised. I was immunised as a child as a matter of routine—my parents, a doctor and nurse, had seen first-hand the effects of lethal diseases against which we hope to protect children by immunising them. To my mind there is no doubt that immunising your child vastly increases the odds of a healthy, productive life, and that public health programmes like the national immunisation drive are one of the major advantages of living now, and not in the eighteenth century.

Breastfeeding vs bottle-feeding

* There is a tonne of research and anecdotal evidence to support breastfeeding. There really is no doubt: breastfeeding is the best nutritional start you can give your baby. Add to this the attendant advantages of fostering the mother–child bond and giving you a reason to regularly sit on

your duff and relax, and it's not surprising your midwife, GP, Plunket nurse and best friend will all encourage you to give it a go, even if it hurts. Developmental molecular biologist John Medina describes breast milk as a magic bullet that makes babies smarter, delivering salts, vitamins and immunity that can't be found anywhere else. New British research from Oxford University and the University of Essex found children who had been breastfed for as little as four weeks as babies did better on cognitive tests—reading, writing and mathematics—at age five, seven, eleven and fourteen.

* If you choose to breastfeed, it is generally agreed that you should aim to keep at it for at least six months. The American Paediatric Association advises mothers to breastfeed exclusively for the first six months and continue with a combination of solids and mother's milk until the child is at least one year old. If breastfeeding still works for the child and mother at that point, there is no reason to stop, because there is nutritional value in breastfeeding for as long as it continues.

* What of mothers who for whatever reason cannot or do not breastfeed? Sadly, they often feel like failures and experience tremendous guilt for not being able to provide their baby with the benefits of breastmilk. Being told by complete strangers that they should be trying harder to breastfeed is not helpful—it's plain annoying. It is not for nothing that these women speak of the 'Breastapo'. Reasons women don't breastfeed include mastitis—a very painful breast infection with flu-like symptoms when one

or both breasts becomes engorged with milk—blocked milk ducts, inability to produce enough milk to sustain the baby, and exhaustion. Making milk and spending up to an hour at a time for each feed—sometimes several times each day—requires a lot of energy. A mother who is struggling to cope with the physical demands of raising an infant may need to supplement her milk with formula, or resort to using it exclusively.

* We are lucky to live in an age when a good substitute to mother's milk is available. Formula, a combination of cow's milk protein, vegetable oils, minerals and vitamins, was developed to save lives. It used to be that mothers who couldn't breastfeed didn't just feel inadequate, they had to hand their babies over to wet nurses for feeding, or watch them die from malnutrition and dehydration, then termed a 'failure to thrive'. When formula became available in the 1930s it was a miracle product. In fact, mothers were so enamoured of it that breastfeeding rates dropped dramatically as 'modern' mums delighted in mixing up batches of faux milk for their babies. Now there is a whiff of shame associated with trundling down the supermarket aisle where one finds those shiny tins of formula, which goes to show you how many of these iron-clad mothering 'truths' are little more than fads.

* Either way you go, you will probably hear about it for better or worse. For example, Joy, a mother of three, was chastised by a stranger for bottle-feeding her third child, who was unaware that she had no choice, because she was on medication that tainted her milk.

> * While as a culture we are very breast-milk happy, there are still some dinosaurs out there who will get uncomfortable when you feed your little one in public. Ninety per cent of them are men of a certain age. They will say it's inappropriate, or stare at your chest reflexively simply because it's there and despite the fact that a small person is attached to it. Many restaurants and cafes are not particularly well set up for breastfeeding mothers who prefer privacy and you may find yourself perching awkwardly on a toilet lid, or leaning against a sink to feed. This is where malls have staked out their territory as the mummy-friendliest public spaces around, boasting parents' rooms with screened-off feeding cubicles, clocks, roomy toilet stalls and changing tables. If you are not prepared to consign yourself to a mall existence, then I say find a quiet corner at your favourite cafe/restaurant or a park bench and do what you need to do. If anyone is crass enough to say something directly to you, a dignified 'My baby is hungry' should suffice.

I would have to say that even amongst the general population the national mood is very much in favour of mother's milk. It is wonderful that we have taken up the breastfeeding challenge with such alacrity. So many people asked me if I was breastfeeding my son. Often as not, an affirmative was met with a 'good on you' or 'well done', which was positive and supportive, which makes a nice change. Obviously the 'Breast is Best' public campaign has worked well, because there is wide understanding that breast milk is better for an infant's brain development, emotional security and early resistance to bugs. And for the budget-minded, it is no small advantage that mother's milk is free. Just keep feeding mama good food and baby is set.

Stay-at-home vs go to work

* Is there anything more damaging, and frankly insulting, to mothers and women in general than this ridiculous fake war between women who stay at home with their children and those who go out to work? I got so steamed up about it that I wrote a separate chapter, see 'Those blasted mummy wars'.

* In a nutshell, not every woman gets to choose whether she works or stays at home. It is very often a circumstance that is thrust upon her. Usually there are financial imperatives which demand that a mother work—because she is a high earner and the mortgage needs to be paid, for example. The same goes for the stay-at-home mum—she might find if she worked that she would spend all her pay on childcare, making work of nil benefit.

* Some women want to work outside the home even if there is no financial gain because they like to use their professional skills and interact with adults.

* Other women believe so passionately in their role as early educators and nurturers that they can't bear the thought of leaving their children with someone else.

* It is not an easy course to navigate, and that reality is made harder by all the opinions one gets from other people on this issue. Working mothers feel guilty for leaving their

children in someone else's care, and they miss them, too, on a physical level. It actually hurts to be away from baby. Stay-at-home mothers feel guilty for not loving every moment of their precious day with baby. They feel bad when they get bored and snappish.

There are few mothers who have not agonised over this decision and we should all respect everyone's ability to make the right choice for themselves and their families.

Baby routine vs freestyling

* When you take your cute bundle home, your whole notion of a schedule will be thrown into disarray. Babies have their own ideas about when they want to eat, sleep and cuddle up with mum and dad. You can either allow them to take the lead, feeding them on demand, napping when they sleep and fitting everything else in when you can (which means next to never), or you can set a timetable and train your baby to follow it, like a young Weimaraner. Proponents on either side tend to be evangelical about their choice, and deadly dull in their explanations of why they do things the way they do. There are theories and philosophies and products to support each. It's a racket.

* A baby-led routine means you go with the flow, which can be more relaxing as it removes any pressure to be any-where or do anything at a particular time. It also means it can be hard to ever leave the house or actually accom-plish any task, as newborns have no desire to go to the

supermarket or walk round the park or put on a load of dishes. Given a choice, the average infant would probably opt to spend the day gazing at the cobwebs on the ceiling and wiggling their fingers in front of their face.

* Forming a routine is the basis of countless books produced by scheduling gurus who call themselves baby whisperers and parenting coaches and sanity preservers.

* Rather than viewing this choice as indicative of how your life is going to run for the next eighteen years, realise that the first year with a baby is a unique time and the way you choose to organise your days now is not going to determine how you organise your days forever.

I call all those scheduling gurus a pain in the arse, but that's mostly because I was unable to establish a routine until Micah was a year old and I took back control of my life and his. Things may be different if I have another child. A friend of mine who had a baby around the same time as me set a routine the day she returned home after giving birth. She had books and charts and big plans. Witnessing how much she managed to do each day and the immaculate state of her home made me feel like a slug lying fat and slimy in the garden. But, honestly, scheduling was beyond my capabilities at that point.

Nanny vs daycare

* The very word 'nanny' conjures up images of some practical, starched and sexless creature who facilitates your

fabulous life from her headquarters in your spare bedroom above the garage. And costs a bomb.

* Today's nanny is just as likely to be a cute young woman with messy hair and sparkly toenail varnish driving the family tank from music group to the library, all while keeping up a one-sided conversation with her tiny charges and making the dads at baby swim class feel uncomfortable.

* Nanny's services are still pricey, although it is increasingly common for several families to pool together and share a nanny.

* The theory is that small children do better with one loved caregiver rather than multiple, changing staff members at a childcare centre. Children who do not bond with a primary caregiver can suffer anxiety and are unlikely to learn as well as bonded children. They may feel they are not getting enough attention, and begin to hit, bite, throw things and generally act up.

* This is why a lot of parents believe a nanny providing one-on-one care is better for their small child than a daycare centre where there are many children and many caregivers. If you can afford it, nanny care can be wonderful, and you often hear of children who maintain relationships with a loved nanny long after they have moved on to work with another family.

* Daycare can also be positive for a small child—it depends on the daycare centre you choose. Look for one with small numbers that assigns a primary caregiver to each child— someone they can form a trusting bond with and rely on

to change their nappy, put them down for naps, play with them and organise their meals.

* When choosing a daycare centre or a nanny, get a recommendation from someone you trust, visit the centre/meet the nanny, ask lots of questions, and listen to your gut.

Personally, I have found daycare a blessing. Micah loves his two main caregivers and comes home tired and happy having spent the day playing in the sandpit, chasing the resident bunny, painting, running up and down wooden ramps, collecting plastic chains in a little tote he slings over his arm like a handbag, and eating snacks galore. He goes two days a week and that is enough for our family for now, but I wouldn't hesitate to send him more often if the need arose.

Further reading

Brain Rules for Baby: How to Raise a Smart and Happy Child from Zero to Five, by John Medina, Pear Press, 2010

Living Green: The New Zealand handbook for an eco-friendly, toxin-free, sustainable life by Annmaree Kane and Christina Neubert, New Holland, 2008

'Cloth or Disposables? Half-century debate still on' by Leanne Halie, *Seattle Times*, 4 April 2011

'Breastfeeding aids child brain development, study finds' by Tracy McVeigh, *The Observer*, 13 March 2011

'Before We Are Born', first report from Growing up in New Zealand: A longitudinal study of New Zealand Children and their Families, University of Auckland, 2010

American Academy of Paediatrics at aap.org

Home Birth Aotearoa at homebirth.org.nz

Immunisation Advisory Centre, University of Auckland at immune.org.nz

Natural Resources Defense Council at nrdc.org

'Report on Maternity: Maternity and Newborn Information', Ministry of Health at moh.govt.nz

10. Madonna, the Madonna and me

Mother icons: When I grow up I want to be just like her

When Tom Cruise is a spiritual leader and Carla Bruni is the First Lady of France, we know we live in strange times. Celebrity culture is inescapable. Keith Richards falls out of a tree while holidaying in Fiji and makes the evening news. Sandra Bullock's husband cheats on her and their split generates magazine and newspaper stories for months. Months!

Ours is an age where we have unprecedented access to celebrities' lives—whether we want it or not. Sure, you can avoid gossip magazines and tabloid newspapers, but you'll be watching the evening news, half-heartedly catching up on the interest rate adjustment, and bam!, Angelina Jolie has closed the air space above Namibia to give birth, Madonna has adopted an infant from Malawi who may or not be an actual orphan, and Nicole Kidman has had a surprise second baby with the help of a 'gestational carrier'. It's not news, but it's served up as if it were, with a side dish of smirking scepticism from our news presenters, who really should know better.

Deborah, mother of two, has strong feelings on the subject:

> Media depictions of celebrity mothers are a load of toss
> and so misleading to normal women leading normal
> lives. I think a lot of celebrity mothers are very narcissistic and this will be very bad for the children.

We know what books celebrities read, what fashion designers they like, who they vote for, where they holiday, what they think about global warming, what diets they follow, what cars they drive and which rehab facility they favour. It's creepy. And with the rise of the reality television star, more and more ordinary people are becoming famous and reaping the often dubious rewards: gymnasium-like houses, limited-edition cars, invitations to fancy parties, constant attention, and a sense of inflated self-importance. When someone as unremarkable as Paris Hilton can become a 'star', you start to believe that anyone can. And when you get such an intimate glimpse of the life these very unspecial people lead, you naturally start to think you can lead that life, too.

Without even realising that we are doing it, in Auckland and New Plymouth and Gisborne and Nelson, we aspire to lead scaled-down versions of the evidently fabulous lives led by celebrities. We model our eating and dress habits on people who are famous—some of them for no logical reason at all—and we aspire to own homes like theirs, or at least a

$15,000 sofa like the one Cameron Diaz lounges on panther-like in *InStyle* magazine. We get child-substitute dogs like our favourite celebs, we force our sisters and best friends to fashion crystal-studded favours inspired by Jennifer Lopez's weddingpalooza, we buy the same 'cult' jeans as Kate Beckinsale, we expect special treatment like our idols. When celebrity relationships fall apart, or they are photographed coming out of Starbucks with frappuccino sludge all over their t-shirts, we feel reassured that they are just like us, after all. This obsessive love–hate relationship with our chosen deities is the twenty-first century version of the gladiator games and it's every bit as sick and twisted. And yet, each week I buy my copy of *NW* magazine to tee-hee at plastic surgery gone wrong, gowns poorly accessorised on the red carpet, and the torrid make-up–break-up cycle.

Call us stupid, and I suspect future generations will, but we also take parenting cues from celebrities. No wonder we are struggling. When I was pregnant I wanted one of those trendy baby slings, so I could go about my business of tidying the kitchen, doing laundry, reading Important Books, strolling the neighbourhood, etcetera, with my little munchkin sleeping soundly as he listened to my heartbeat, soothed into a blissful state of contentedness. It would be my hands-free baby kit. I researched slings online and found a company that made reversible ones in cool retro-inspired fabrics that had been used by not-annoying celebrity mothers such as Gwen Stefani and Naomi Watts. Did I want the sling used by Gwen Stefani? Hell, yeah! So I hunted one down and bought it: brown paisley on one side, orange and pink cherry blossoms on the other. Great excitement when it arrived in the mail and I tried it on, shoving a teddy bear in to pose as baby. It was awkward with my big pregnant belly in the way, so Tim tried it on, except he one-upped me by cosying the smiling dog into the sling. I took a picture of them then hung the sling on the back of Micah's door, awaiting his arrival, and my arrival as a fashionably casual sling-wearing mother.

Imagine the thrill when I had a real live baby to pop into my sling and could do my Domestic Goddess bit with the laundry and the sleeping baby and mummy's soothing heartbeat et al. Problem was I couldn't get Micah arranged in such a way that his breathing wasn't compromised or his big bobble-head at risk. Either his chin was forced to rest on his chest, which cut off his oxygen supply, or he flopped about on my shoulder, breathing freely but with inadequate head support. I put the sling away for a couple of months until he grew into it, but by then I was having back pain from lifting Micah and the increasingly needy Scout, as well as hunching forward while breastfeeding around the clock. It's a common problem for new mothers. Tucking Micah in the sling and wearing him, while comforting for us both, ached too much for me to do it for more than five minutes at a time, and given all the faffing required to settle him comfortably in the sling for that five minutes of mummy-and-me time I gave up, rock star aspirations forgotten.

It was the same thing with the nappy bag. I was not going to carry around a bag for the next three years emblazoned with rattles and baby animals, I declared. I wanted something chic, something Naomi Watts wouldn't be ashamed to be seen with. An exhaustive search produced a large reversible bag that looks like an ordinary tote bag except it has multiple pockets and extra, smaller bags you can attach to it for keeping bottles cool and soiled nappies safely sealed off from the public nose. It cost a bomb and I hate it. Not because it isn't chic and practical because it is both, and durable too, but because I have to take it everywhere I go and I am sick of the sight of it. It wouldn't matter if I was carrying a garbage sack or a $3000 'It bag' every day, I would tire of it.

Despite our best efforts to ignore mummy icons, even the ridiculous ones, I believe they do have an impact on us—not on how we choose to mother our own children, but on our expectations of the experience. In the past sixty years pregnancy has gone from being a private affair, with baby bellies kept under wraps and pregnant women often semi-sequestered at home, to a shout-it-from-the-rooftops celebration. A lot of that is due to the celebrity fad for getting pregnant five minutes before the fertility window of opportunity slams shut, getting papped buying chi-chi baby furniture, and talking ad nauseam about how fulfilling the whole experience is and how it has forced the new mother to take stock of her life and realise what is truly important, yada yada yada. And that is a good thing, mostly.

But the drive to then lose the pregnancy weight in a trifle and strut around in a string bikini while toting an outsized baby who looks like they could eat mama for breakfast, and to proclaim (while neglecting to acknowledge the staff who help facilitate it) how naturally motherhood comes to them, is decidedly not a good thing. As Gillian, mother of three, comments:

For goodness sake, I'm sure if I could afford a night nanny and housekeeper, I too could say motherhood is all good with no downside.

Unfortunately, the rise of the celebrity mother has led women with far less privileged lives to think they too should deny the fact that they have just produced a baby by shrinking their bodies with haste and attempting to get on with life as it was pre-baby—which when you think about it is a self-loathing sort of thing to do. Once you've had a baby you can't behave as if you haven't got a baby, and really, why would you want to? Becoming a mother leaves marks on your heart and your body, and that is okay. Remember, you will not get out of this life unscathed.

I was a highly impressionable little girl when Princess Diana got married. As a special never-to-be-repeated treat, I was allowed to stay up past 8 pm to watch the wedding, to see Kiri Te Kanawa sing, and to fall instantly in love with that frothy monstrosity of a train—eight metres of vain hope and optimism. My mother bought me a little blue Ladybird book about Diana, which pictured her as an elbowy child hugging a rabbit, and later as a willowy royal girlfriend fleeing paparazzi with hair in her eyes. I thought she was unbearably wonderful—a sweet slice of fairy-tale loveliness. I loved her Austin Mini Metro and her crazy old-lady hats and her sapphire engagement ring. I loved her journey from kindy teacher to princess. So when Diana had children, I took notice of that, too.

Remember when Charles and Diana brought Prince

William to New Zealand and he crawled around on a blanket at Government House and played with a Buzzy Bee? And many years later, when Diana took her boys on beach holidays and rode with them on roller coasters and lay with them in the grass at the polo? Diana's seemingly casual, natural mothering style became a marker for women to measure themselves against. When she died, her boys requested a 'Mummy' bouquet accompany the funeral cortège and nations swooned. She was, as far as admirers could tell, the real deal: a treasured mother-figure whose loving arms extended towards AIDS patients, sick children and the homeless. She was beautiful and good. Possibly a little kooky, but great with kids.

Today's Princess Diana, although her crown is slipping fast, would have to be Angelina Jolie, obsessive collector of children from all over the world. For Ange, motherhood has been a boon to the image, a chance to soften the effect of the tattoos and blood-vial necklace and aggressive man-hunting. She is an unusually gorgeous pregnant woman, even when carrying twins, which can make some women look like they are trying to smuggle small hostages across borders. From extensive media coverage of her life as a mother, we 'know' that she employs 25 staff to keep her brood fed and cared for, that the kids eat a lot of sweets and are allowed to swear, that daughter Shiloh prefers to dress as a boy and call herself John. We don't approve, but the circus-ring parenting is mitigated in the eyes of the press—somewhat—by her role as a UN goodwill ambassador.

In the same way, we develop firm views on other famous

mothers with whom we can compare ourselves. Jennifer Garner is a wholesome, old-fashioned mother, often photographed with her daughters at the playground. Gwyneth Paltrow, Kate Moss and Cate Blanchett are stylish mothers, slim and immaculate. Madonna is a staunch mother—mess with her and you put your life at risk. She is the 'mama grizzly' Sarah Palin wishes she could be.

Every day we are exposed to representations of motherhood that do not reflect the reality of our lives. Famous mothers who wear three-inch stilettos throughout their pregnancy (thanks, Catherine Zeta-Jones), who shed the baby weight within weeks of giving birth (take a bow, Gisele Bündchen), who appear at press events looking fresh and perky when they are supposedly mothering two under-fives without professional assistance (pick a name). And while it is interesting to see how other women handle their pregnancies and new motherhood, it's not actually helpful if they appear to be breezing through it while we are stewing in our own juices and contemplating throwing our children out the window.

Mother-of-one Jo remembers comparing herself unfavourably to famous 'yummy mummies' with their high-performance strollers and tight-fitting maternity clothes and feeling 'utterly inadequate and paranoid' as she mothered her baby. It's easy to get sucked into this vortex of negative comparison, especially when you meet other mothers who are sporting Jennifer Aniston's hair, Gwyneth Paltrow's abs and a reasonable facsimile of one of the Beckham tots.

Deborah, mother of two, says she pays attention to

celebrity mothers 'only to yell at the TV and throw pictures of blimmin' Nicole Kidman across the room' while Sarah, mother of two, says, 'It's part of that culture that feeds the "perfect mother" curse which afflicts mere mortals. It also creates really unhealthy focus around weight.' Mother of two Jackie believes there is a lot more pressure on mothers to be 'yummy' than there was a decade ago, which cannot be a good thing. We're not Popsicles, for pity's sake, and we don't come in different flavours. What a vile notion, and yet there it is, served up again and again in the media we consume.

In her thesis paper 'Yummy Mummy?: (Re)Appearance of the Maternal Body in Popular Women's Magazines in New Zealand', Deborah Taylor of Victoria University of Wellington found that media representations of the postnatal body were beginning to have negative effects on mothers' well-being after giving birth. Her research concluded that women who dieted and exercised their way back to pre-pregnancy form quickly were celebrated for being 'sexy' and 'healthy' while the ordinary post-pregnancy body (ie doughy) was depicted as 'undisciplined' and 'unattractive' and therefore undesirable. Ordinary mothers are supposedly getting things wrong. As American writer Erin McClellan put it in her article 'The Mass Media and its Depiction of Mothers':

Unfortunately for women today, the media has an insatiable obsession with motherhood. These idealised accounts of blissful superhuman mothers permeate media outlets, continually excluding millions of women from their narrow definition of good mothers.

While most women surveyed for this book said they were unaffected by the celebrity mother phenomenon, each was aware of what celebrity mothers represented in modern culture and, despite themselves, they knew quite a lot about Angelina and Victoria and Heidi. Not one of them thought this was a positive development.

If they showed any genuine interest in celebrity mothers it was to do with time management. Dita, mother of two, says:

I wonder how they manage to keep down their fabulous careers and still be good mothers. Does a lot of in-home care affect the child or are the kids completely fine, and I'm the one smothering my kids with attention perhaps?

Melissa, mother of two, says:

If anything I feel empathy for celebrity mums with the pressure to lose weight and look perfect within weeks of giving birth. What I do find interesting is how successful women have juggled the demands of family and career, especially women who have done very well in business.

Fiona, mother of two, said the only media mothers she took any notice of were television characters Marge Simpson and Lois from *Malcolm in the Middle*:

I love how they both try so hard to get it right in the face of all sorts of exasperations, difficulties and distractions—just like real mums.

If celebrity mothers are nothing more than a diverting spectacle, more troubling are media depictions of mothers as idealised traditional homebodies or über-successful professionals in glamorous fields when very few women are either. Caryl Rivers, a professor of journalism at Boston University, in her book *Selling Anxiety: How the News Media Scare Women*, sums it up:

> As statistics tell us that more women are getting more college degrees, more MBAs, more MDs, the more intense becomes the message that this is all a terrible mistake, that only by returning to traditional lives can women find true happiness. It's the media's main message to women and it gets played over and over again.

And yet, here we have a 'high-profile boutique owner' speaking to *W* magazine in an article titled 'Born yesterday' by Emily Holt, about the speed with which working mothers are returning to the workforce after having children. 'I don't know anybody who is taking three months off anymore,' she says glibly. 'You can be tired at home or tired at the Balenciaga showroom.' Which is no more realistic, desirable or helpful to the average mother than the idea that she must move to Stepford and make peerless apricot jam and feather-light scones, or balance an A-list acting career with child-rearing.

Where are the media depictions of 'regular' women leading 'normal' lives, you might ask? They exist, but they can be hard to find, and that is because journalists, by the nature of their jobs, focus on the unusual, the special, the tragic, the era-defining. And generally, that's not you and me, mixing up another batch of formula or bleaching the toilet.

When you look at the icons of mothering, you find a group of women who are often captured in the public memory during their most trying times, doomed to forever be sad or stoic or sexually undeveloped. Of the holy Madonna (as opposed to the whorey Madonna) we understand that she was meek and mild, a simple, virtuous woman chosen by God to carry his child. She is not a major player in the Bible, but she is celebrated for her unquestioning devotion to her God and her pivotal role in raising his son. The Catholic Church has put her right at the centre of its belief system. Her pureness and goodness, while impressive, are not possible for other mothers to emulate—after all, hers was the only immaculate conception.

Political mother Jackie Kennedy maintained a chilly dignity after the death of her husband that inspired great respect and raised two apparently decent and talented children, but she blew it when she hooked up with Greek billionaire Aristotle Onassis. He was just too tanned and oily for her public to embrace. 'Good' mothers, I find, aren't generally entitled to a second act.

An iconic mother, for all the wrong reasons, Joan Crawford's angry parenting style was immortalised in the exposé *Mommie Dearest*, written by her adopted daughter, Christina. She depicted Joan as an alcoholic harpy with an obsession for neatness and cleanliness. The new Joan is Yale law professor Amy Chua, whose controversial memoir *Battle Hymn of the Tiger Mother* compares Western and Eastern parenting styles and claims Chinese parents tend to produce more successful children because they ride them like those little donkeys that carry tourists to the bottom of the Grand Canyon. No play dates, no sleepovers, no after-school activities, no mucking around. This sounds boring but not damaging until you learn that Chua punished her three-year-old by making her stand outside in the freezing cold and called her older daughter 'garbage' when she disrespected her. She admits herself that she took her philosophy too far, and claims she was writing partly in jest, but it is too late. The entire world thinks she is a nut job.

Fictional mothers to whom we might look for guidance are often fairly one-dimensional, with selflessness a common theme. Marmee from *Little Women* is saint-like in her acceptance of the family's reduced circumstances and her nuggety resourcefulness when Father goes off to fight in the American Civil War. She does not complain and she does not waver in her faith that Father will return, and her strength is inspirational for her daughters. Ellen O'Hara from *Gone With the Wind* is such a do-gooder that she catches typhoid from a 'white trash' family to whom she is ministering and dies. Her memory taunts Scarlett for years as she wishes she could be the same kind of 'great lady' her mother had been.

Shirley Partridge from *The Partridge Family* is relentlessly positive, reliable, and always ready with a word of advice. She is pretty and perfect and ultimately pretty perfectly dull. In fact, that description goes for many television mothers, from Marion Cunningham (*Happy Days*) to Elyse Keaton (*Family Ties*) to Debra Barone (*Everybody Loves Raymond*). Clair

Huxtable of the *Cosby Show* was my first glimpse at a professional working mother who shared an equal status with her husband and enjoyed herself immensely, and I admired her despite the architectural 80s shoulder pads. But the Cosbys' situation was not typical—she was a lawyer, her husband a doctor in private practice, and they had resources at their disposal that are not available to most.

When asked who influences their mothering, most women surveyed for this book said their own mother was the key figure to whom they looked for guidance in how to mother well. Dita, mother of two, says:

My mother was—in my opinion—an excellent mother. Kind and caring, not overly permissive but she completely loved being at home with us when we were little. I try and be like her, but I also have a generous dollop of my father in there—impatient. I have tried the earth-mother routine but have finally admitted defeat several years down the track!

Maria, mother of two, says:

I guess the person I try, and usually fail, to be like is my sister-in-law. She is amazing—so warm and kind but very, very funny. She jokes a lot with her kids and has the right proportions of humour and firmness. I will never be like her but when in doubt I think, 'How would she handle this?' I guess also, in a less conscious way, I model my mum, in the sense that my answer to everything is to hug and tell my kids I love them. I was never short on that. I have to say she was also alternately full of praise and criticism and I try not to be like that but don't always succeed. 'I'm telling you this because I love you' is a well-used phrase and it has to stop.

Jackie, mother of two, says:

I am a very different kind of mother from my own mother and my husband's mother. I am a lot more liberated and much more of a friend to my children. I think I'm pretty laid back compared to most parents and it seems the boys' friends think so, too, as our house is always crammed with other people's kids. However I am also extremely protective of my boys, probably too much so. I guess when you've already lost a child it kind of makes you like that. If there is one thing I learned from my mother which I have carried through to my own children it's to keep the lines of communication open.

Whether we think they did a fantastic job or not, our mothers taught us how to mother—through their good example and when we react against what we didn't like about our own childhoods. It is their example that endures, even while we try to push away gossipy snippets about Jessica Alba's post-baby workout plan or Reese Witherspoon's perspective on child discipline.

I remember the things my mother did to make me feel cared for—the fulsome lunchboxes, the toast slices stamped 'I love you', the trips to McDonald's after ballet class (I was never going to be an ethereal Odette). Come to think of it, they all revolve around food, a point that makes me smile when I am punching out slices of cheese for Micah in the shape of trains. 'Train cheese' is usually served on crackers, but not long ago my mother gave me her 'I love you' toast stamp, which means I have options.

Further reading

Battle Hymn of the Tiger Mother by Amy Chua, Bloomsbury Publishing, 2011

Mommie Dearest by Christina Crawford, Berkley Publishing Group, 1979

Gone with the Wind by Margaret Mitchell, Macmillan, 1936

Little Women by Louisa May Alcott, Roberts Brothers, 1868

'Retreat of the "Tiger Mother"' by Kate Zernike, *New York Times*, 14 January 2011

11. Worry, my new state of mind

Pregnancy complications, postnatal depression, cot death,
meningitis, toddler accidents

Mothering is synonymous with worry: it taps into wells of
unease you didn't know lay within you, and whips up storms
of anxiety. As I understand it, 'worry' and 'mother' actually
sit together in the modern dictionary, and I am not alone, as
Angela, mother of one, explains:

> There is always something to worry about when you
> have a child. These worries change as the child grows
> older, but there is always something in the back of my
> mind. I expect this will carry on until I'm old and dod-
> dery and he has long since become capable of looking
> after himself.

Some of your concerns will be well-founded and reasoned,
others will be pure emotion—reactions to the intense love

you have for your child. Your baby is small and defenceless and you are hard-wired to protect her to the best of your abilities, but remember, statistics are on your side: most babies born into families in the Western world make it through early childhood and beyond just fine. Medically, there has never been a better time to be a baby. But we all know someone who wasn't lucky, we all have heard horror stories and we all worry.

I think it is useful to separate the uncommon, bad-stroke-of-luck scenarios from those most likely to affect you. In this chapter, I highlight some common problems that occur in pregnancy, post-pregnancy and in the first two years of a child's life.

Miscarriage

We flew to Paraguay hugging the secret of our pregnancy. I did all the good-girl things that are supposed to help protect your foetus: I eliminated caffeine and alcohol, I got lots of sleep, I was careful about what I ate. I couldn't do anything about the enervating heat or the go-go-go schedule.

We were in Paraguay, rarely top of anyone's South American must-do list, to see if we could find the isolated communist settlement where my grandmother was born. It was a late nineteenth-century attempt at establishing Utopia on a flood plain; my great-grandparents were among a band of hopefuls from Australia and England who believed you could leave greed and material concerns behind with the banks and courthouses of English-style civilisation; that if everyone pooled their resources, worked like packhorses, and sang lots of uplifting workers' ditties, they would find enlightenment. It didn't work, of course, and my family were lucky to finally get out. I'd always loved the stories about their odyssey, and the fact that they'd tried such a thing in the first place.

It had been a dream of mine to go to Cosme ever since I was a child hearing stories about the flock of great-aunts and great-uncles who ran wild in the monte, playing pirates among the trees, picking limes and eating them straight off the tree sliced and sprinkled with salt. Dances at the hall, where my great-grandmother and the other women wore bright fireflies in their hair, trapped in small pieces of net attached to hair pins. Men riding around on their horses playing explorer while the women cleaned, cooked, tended children, cared for the ill, and plotted their way back to the English-speaking world and conveniences such as electricity and running water.

So, despite the fact that I would be scooting around a completely foreign place in 35-degree heat in my first trimester of a much-anticipated first pregnancy, I wasn't about to call off the trip. I was a fit, healthy woman with no known medical conditions and a future mapped out for my little offshoot—and I was the great-granddaughter of a woman who spent thirteen years in Paraguay, birthing children and keeping them safe. Bring it on.

It was on the way back to the United States, somewhere over the Pacific, that things went wrong. Or rather things had probably always been wrong with that pregnancy, but it was on our LAN flight that the bleeding began. I was nine and a half weeks pregnant, still within the twelve-week period when you are advised not to announce your pregnancy to one and all because miscarriage risk is highest. We hadn't said a word to anyone. Having bought several books on pregnancy and shoved them in my carry-on bag, I knew that at nine weeks a foetus is about the size of an olive, that the ears are formed and it can move its limbs.

In a Los Angeles emergency room I was scanned and it was clear that it was not a viable pregnancy, that this little olive was not going to survive. The attending doctor told me it was not my fault, that there was nothing I did to cause this, and I appreciated her kindness. I do still wonder, though, if exposing myself to unaccustomed tropical summer heat and eating foods containing unknown ingredients may have put my foetus at risk. It's not something I can ever know, but will likely nag at me for the rest of my life.

Because I did not have health insurance (the ER trip cost over US$1000, and writing the cheque for that was a bitter pill), it was decided that a dilation and curettage procedure to surgically remove all pregnancy tissue to avoid infection, while desirable, was not necessary and I was sent home. Back in San Francisco, I spent five days in bed, waiting for the miscarriage to take its natural course. The pain was surprising, lots of cramping and general achiness. Afterwards I felt completely empty.

Miscarriages are common, far more so than most people realise. For every woman who knows she is pregnant, there is a 10–20 per cent chance the pregnancy will end in miscarriage—80 per cent of those in the first twelve weeks. Many more women miscarry in the very early part of pregnancy before they even realise they are pregnant, and it is disguised as a heavy period. Usually miscarriage is the result of an abnormality in the foetus—something is dramatically wrong with it. That doesn't make it any less upsetting.

Age is a major risk factor. There's a 25 per cent chance a pregnant woman aged 30–39 will miscarry. For pregnant women aged 40–44 the rate rises to 50 per cent. Having a miscarriage also raises your risk of having subsequent miscarriages.

There are many ways you can reduce your risk of miscarriage, and certainly they are worth doing, for your peace of mind as well as your health:

* Avoid raw meats and cheeses that can harbour listeria.
* Maintain a healthy weight prior to conceiving.
* Stop smoking.
* Avoid second-hand smoke.
* Limit your caffeine intake.
* Avoid alcohol.
* Don't use drugs.
* Check your prescription medications with your doctor.
* Avoid extreme temperatures.
* Don't lift heavy objects.
* Avoid contact sports.

Despite the common occurrence of miscarriage, I have found that people don't really talk about it, or know what to say when they hear that someone has experienced one. It can often be considered a small loss, not something to grieve about, but three years after mine I still mourn the loss of that foetus and the possibility of a child, even though I went on to have a healthy little boy a year later. It hit me much harder than I anticipated and I am not unique in this. For information and comfort, try Miscarriage Support Auckland, miscarriagesupport.org.nz.

Other pregnancy complications

Without wishing to be alarmist, there are a number of other pregnancy complications that can make the experience challenging for you and your baby, and can endanger your life and theirs. When you are pregnant it is worth learning a little about these conditions so you can ensure they are not affecting you, or recognise symptoms if they do. Your midwife or doctor should be your first call if you suspect you may be developing any of the following conditions.

Pre-eclampsia: This is the combination of elevated blood pressure and protein in the urine. Women over 35, those carrying more than one foetus, and those with a history of high blood pressure, kidney disease or diabetes are at a higher risk of developing pre-eclampsia, which can lead to an early induced delivery, or a long period of bed rest for the expectant mother. It can be life threatening and occurs in three to five per cent of pregnancies. New Zealand Action on Pre-eclampsia was founded by Wendy Roberts, after her experience with the condition. Go to www.nzapec.com.

Gestational diabetes: This usually develops in the second trimester, when an expectant mother is not producing enough insulin (the hormone that moves sugar from the blood into the cells, where it is used for energy). Gestational diabetes can be controlled through diet and medication and disappears as soon as the baby is born. However, it increases the mother's chances of developing Type 2 diabetes later in life and in subsequent pregnancies. It can also result in a very large baby, complicating the birth, who may suffer a dangerously low blood glucose level soon after birth. For more information, go to www.diabetes.org.nz.

Ectopic pregnancy: This is when a fertilised egg implants itself outside the uterus, in the fallopian tube, ovary, or cervix, for example. Pregnancy can't continue when this happens and needs to be terminated for the mother's health. Risk factors include getting pregnant while using an IUD (intrauterine device) and having an STI (sexually transmitted infection) such as chlamydia. Symptoms to watch out for are dizziness, extreme pelvic pain and bleeding. If you need support after terminating an ectopic pregnancy, go to www.miscarriagesupport.org.nz.

Placenta previa: This is when the placenta is lying unusually low in the uterus, and is close to or covering the cervix. It is not a problem in early pregnancy and often the placenta will 'move' on its own (it is attached to the uterus so does not actually shift, but its position in relation to the cervix changes as the uterus grows). However, placenta previa in late pregnancy can cause bleeding and may require an extended period of bed rest and/or early delivery of the baby, usually by caesarian.

Oligohydramnios: This is when the amniotic sac protecting the baby does not contain enough fluid. It affects 4–8 per cent of pregnant women and may require induced delivery. Signs of oligohydramnios include a foetus measuring small for its stage and a mother feeling few baby movements.

Antenatal depression: Around ten per cent of women suffer from depression when they are pregnant. The symptoms are the same as postnatal depression, but antidepressant medication is preferably not prescribed to a pregnant woman. Depending on the severity of symptoms, talk therapy can be helpful. Talk to your doctor or midwife if you think you may be depressed.

Post-pregnancy complications

Postnatal depression: Between ten and fifteen per cent of mothers experience postnatal depression (PND), making it far more common than many people realise. It also suggests every coffee or play group in the country probably has at least one member who has suffered or is suffering from postnatal depression. Despite that, there is still a sense of failure associated with PND and women who have just had a baby feel they should be happy and grateful, not overwhelmed and sad. Instead of seeing PND as a condition that affects many women, is treatable, and is no reflection on their abilities as a mother, women often see it as a sign of personal weakness or failure.

The symptoms of PND can easily be confused with the aftermath of a baby's arrival in the home: exhaustion, decreased energy, a change in appetite, difficulty concentrating, a change in sleeping patterns, feeling anxious or trapped, loneliness, guilt, hopelessness. Every new mother is going to feel one or more of these emotions. In fact, the infamous 'baby blues' that hit in the first week after birth guarantee she will cry for no apparent reason at least once or twice when she takes her baby home. But the 'baby blues' only last a few days and PND is a far more serious complaint that can last six months or more if untreated.

Reasons for onset include a difficult birth, a premature or sick baby, difficulties breastfeeding, lack of a supportive partner, social isolation, and a history of depression.

It can be difficult for families and partners to know how to approach a woman with PND, who will likely try to give the impression that she's coping well and does not need help. Depression saps a person's confidence and ability to clearly analyse her situation and she will not thank anyone for stating what seems obvious to them. Tough love is not the answer, reminding her of her blessings is not the answer, ignoring her moods is not the answer.

Treatment for PND includes talk therapy and medication, rest, gentle exercise, a healthy diet, and social contact. There is a tonne of information available on the website www.mothersmatter.co.nz, run by the Postnatal Depression Family/Whanau Trust.

Heather, mother of three, suffered postnatal depression after having her first child. The family had just moved city, she knew few people, her husband was working long hours in a new job, and she had just given up work to stay home with an infant. She remembers:

I really didn't cope. In the end when everything got too much, I headed north with my baby to spend a week with my mother. I did this a couple of times over the first year. When my daughter was eleven months old I went back to work part-time and life seemed to balance itself out again. I didn't have the same problems after the next two.

Angela's postnatal depression was more severe. She needed constant support and medication to help her through the first months of her son's life:

I had to go on antidepressants and have almost round-the-clock psychiatric nursing. A nurse came to help me look after the baby during the day from about 9 am–4 pm and then another nurse would come from 10 pm–7 am to look after him so that I could sleep. I was also in a support group for mothers with post-natal depression and had to see a psychiatrist. My self-esteem hit rock bottom because I felt like I was doing a bad job of being a mother.

Like Heather, Angela came out the other side but she believes general awareness of PND is still low.

Post-traumatic stress disorder (PTSD): Most commonly associated with soldiers returning from war zones or survivors of natural disasters, PTSD also affects women who have experienced a difficult birth. Symptoms include anxiety, panic attacks, flashbacks to the birth and an inability to move past the experience. If that applies to you, go see your doctor. The charitable trust Trauma and Birth Stress, www.tabs.org.nz, provides New Zealand mothers with information about post-traumatic stress disorder in relation to pregnancy and birth.

Cot death: Now known in New Zealand as SUDI (Sudden Unexpected Death in Infancy), cot death is the unexplained death of a sleeping infant up to one year old. It is most common in babies aged two to four months, and in males (approximately 60 per cent of babies with SUDI are male). Rates are significantly higher among Maori and Pacific Islanders. In New Zealand there are between 60 and 80 cot deaths each year, and SUDI remains the main cause of baby death in the first year of life.

Risk factors include putting a baby down to sleep on its stomach, not breastfeeding, co-sleeping (families sleeping together in one bed), and a home in which someone smokes. It is also considered advisable to remove all toys and pillows from cots, avoid putting babies to sleep on sheepskins, and not to use cot 'bumpers', the fabric panels attached to the bars of the cot to stop draughts and protect the baby from bumps and bruises. Excess blankets and heat are not considered good for sleeping babies.

Factors which lower the SUDI risk include having a

separate sleeping area for babies, the use of dummies, breastfeeding, and putting babies to sleep on their backs. Inconclusive studies have linked SUDI with the chemicals used to make mattresses fire safe, which are said to inter-act with fungus and produce a fatal toxic nerve gas. Dr Jim Sprott, a chemist, advises parents to buy mattresses that don't contain phosphorus, arsenic or antimony or to wrap cot mattresses in thick plastic coverings to avoid these gases leaching out into the baby's air supply. However, the Ministry of Health does not support mattress wrapping.

The SUDI Working Group believes New Zealand could reduce its cot deaths by 60 a year if all babies had their own safe sleeping place, and other risk factors were eliminated. New Zealand has served as a case study for international cot death researchers. In the 1980s and 90s we had one of the highest rates of cot death in the OECD. A national campaign to put babies to sleep on their backs is credited with reducing the rate from around 250 babies per year to about 80 per year.

Meningococcal disease: It is a frightening, fast-moving disease that can be hard to detect given that its onset is similar to the flu. Every winter there are a plethora of cautionary news stories on meningococcal disease and I hesitate to even mention it because of the hysteria it inspires. Once epidemic in New Zealand, it is still a killer that strikes fear in the hearts of parents everywhere, and if you are anything like me you will be always aware of its signs and symptoms. Meningococcal disease was at its worst in 2001, the year there were 370 reported cases and eighteen deaths. Spread by kissing, coughing and sharing drinking vessels, it is most common in babies and children aged five and under, 16–25 year olds and people over 55.

The government campaign to immunise youngsters against meningococcal disease began in 2004 and it is partly credited with the end of the epidemic, although critics argue the epidemic was already on the wane. The MeNZB vaccine was controversial, like vaccinations in general, and some parents refused point blank to allow their kids to be vaccinated. MeNZB is no longer given to babies as a matter of course, but there are supplies in reserve in case of a fresh epidemic.

There are two varieties of the disease: meningitis, which is the inflammation of the linings surrounding the brain, and meningococcal septicaemia, or blood poisoning. Septicaemia is the most serious, and can lead to limb amputations and death. It is meningococcal septicaemia that caused Waiheke Island baby Charlotte Cleverley-Bisman to lose all her limbs as a baby and become a poster child for the immunisation campaign.

Symptoms include high fever, headache, aversion to light, vomiting, stiff neck, and a dark red rash. If you are concerned that your baby may have meningitis or septicaemia, don't hesitate to call 111, call your doctor, or head to your nearest Accident and Emergency clinic. They will not mind checking your little one over, and the peace of mind you will get is invaluable. I speak from a place of hyper-vigilance against all potential baby illnesses—I lie awake worrying about temperatures and sniffly noses and mosquito bites—and I have never once had a negative reaction from medical staff when it comes to examining my boy.

Common baby complaints

Fever: A high temperature—anything over the accepted human range of 36–37.5 degrees Celsius—is usually a sign that the body is fighting an infection. Treatment includes removing extra layers of clothing, ensuring the baby is getting plenty of fluids, applying cold washcloths to the body, and possibly administering paediatric paracetamol. Fever is very common in babies but it can be an indicator of a serious problem. If you are worried, ring PlunketLine (0800 933 922) or see your doctor. Check to make sure your baby is feeding normally and taking an interest in what's going on around her. If not, call your doctor or head to A and E.

Febrile seizures: A high fever (39 degrees or more) can cause convulsions known as febrile seizures. The baby's eyes may roll back, she may vomit, her limbs may go stiff or twitch, and she may lose consciousness. The seizure can last anywhere from a few seconds to fifteen minutes. While frightening to witness, a febrile seizure is usually harmless, although it's a good idea to phone your doctor for advice. While the seizure is ongoing, protect your child's limbs from injury.

Gastric reflux: When babies are said to be 'spilly', meaning they spill or bring up milk after most of their feeds, it is usually because they have gastric reflux. This happens when a valve at the top of the stomach doesn't close properly, allowing the contents of the stomach to return, and while a messy and potentially painful problem, it does not usually require medication. If your refluxy baby is struggling to feed and failing to gain weight, go see your doctor. Advice and support is available at the website cryingoverspiltmilk.co.nz.

Colic: It is still not known what causes the intense, loud crying for extended periods (three hours or more) commonly known as colic. The onset is usually at two to three weeks of age and it is usually gone by three to four months without any intervention required. But while colic is present in your house, it will completely take over. It is incredibly difficult to get anything done or even to think clearly when a baby is screaming, especially when that screaming goes on for hours at a time. It is distressing, too, not knowing how to comfort your colicky baby. Classic remedies include swaddling, jiggling, rubbing the stomach, swinging the baby from side to side, and letting the baby suck a dummy. If you are concerned, your doctor may prescribe medication to ease colic symptoms.

Toddler accidents

By their very nature, toddlers are constantly pushing the boundaries, testing their limits and conquering new tasks which require them to balance on one foot and hang over a ledge while simultaneously reaching for a kettle of boiling water. They can be terrifying to watch, tiny Evil Knievels with no respect for danger. They fall over all the time, they get their hands stuck in doors and drawers, they run towards traffic and will stick anything in their mouths: coins, razor blades, poisonous berries, rusty nails, dog poop. You have to watch them like mother hawks.

Micah was still perfecting his walking when he tripped

and hit his head on the edge of the coffee table. I had been fearing exactly that event for months, had in fact been lobbying to remove the coffee table with its horrible pointy corners from the house, and when the dreaded event came it was actually worse than I'd imagined—despite the small sense of satisfaction I gained from being right about our coffee table's lethal nature. Micah had fallen on his brow bone, which had a long, ugly gash. There was a LOT of blood, his skin blanched to white and he would not stop screaming, which given his devil-may-care nature was the scariest thing of all. We bundled him up into the car and raced to A and E, abandoning our plan to see Spandau Ballet in concert, which was a bummer, actually. He was fine, of course (as soon as we got to A and E he spied the kids' corner and started playing with blocks and cars, even as blood continued to run into his eye), the scar is hardly visible now, and the doctor was nice enough not to make us feel like negligent parents. On a bitter note, apparently Spandau Ballet were *amazing*, and our friends went on about them for months.

Just the other week we had a much bigger scare. We were enjoying a day trip north of Auckland and had stopped at the Matakana Pub on the way home. (I know many parents would not choose to take their toddler to a pub but on this occasion, as on so many others, we did our own thing and it bit us on the arse.) As we sat in the sun in front of the pub and plotted our retirement in Matakana running a hobby vineyard and making soft cheeses, Micah walked along a raised piece of wood and ducked under tables chattering to himself. Then he saw a cat. Micah loves cats. The cat was obviously fairly keen on little boys, too, because she rolled onto her back so he could pat her tummy. Then she got up and padded towards the road, Micah followed and I stood up, ready to fly. 'Micah! Stop!' I yelled, but he kept going, didn't even look back. I ran after him. 'MICAH! STOP RIGHT NOW!' I thundered, but he kept going. I caught him just as he stepped into the gutter.

Scary as this was, the worst part of the experience was how little Micah was affected by it. At this age he understands a lot of what is said to him, and when we explained that he must never, ever go in the road, and that he must always listen when Mummy and Daddy tell him to stop, he shook his head.

I spent the trip back to Auckland trying to impress on him the significance of what had just happened. Twisted round in my seat, I said, 'Micah, when Mummy says stop, you have to stop. Right?'

'No.'

'Yes. When Mummy says stop, you stop.'

'No.' He pushed out his bottom lip and turned his face towards the window.

'Micah, Mummy and Daddy want to keep you safe. If you go in the road you could be hurt. So when Mummy and Daddy say stop, you must stop.'

'Hurt? No!' He started to cry. 'No hurt!'

At this point I probably should have stopped, but I was scared.

'Listen to Mummy. Cars go on the road, and the cars could hurt you. You mustn't go in the road.'

'Cah. Ro-ad.' That got his attention.

'That's right. The road is for cars, not Micah.'

'Mike-ah.'

'So when Mummy says stop, what does Micah do?'

'Go.'

'No! When Mummy says stop Micah must stop!'

'No.'

This went on for the better part of 45 minutes. Micah didn't learn his lesson, but I learned mine. Don't allow yourself to get into an argument with a toddler, and maybe baby leashes aren't so bad after all.

Further reading

Childhood diseases at kidshealth.org.nz

Diabetes New Zealand at diabetes.org.nz

Miscarriage Support Auckland at miscarriagesupport.org.nz

New Zealand Action on Pre-eclampsia at nzapec.com

Postnatal Depression and Family Whanau New Zealand Trust at mothersmatter.co.nz

Trauma and Birth Stress PTSD After Childbirth at tabs.org.nz

12. Time for round two, ding ding!

In which you decide whether you can handle the notion of doing this again

You will have just returned home with your baby—and contrary to popular belief, will not yet have forgotten what an ordeal childbirth is—when well-wishers will lean in close and say conspiratorially, 'So, when are you going to have another one?' And you will want to beat them over the head with the baby bath except, of course, you won't have the energy for it.

Tracey, mother of one, expresses her exasperation:

Why do people keep asking me when we're going to have another? I would never ask anyone that question—it's personal.

It's one of those universal truths, like the rightness of salmon with cream cheese and capers on a bagel, and the goodness of Gandhi and golden labradors. As soon as you have one baby, people will expect you to immediately want another to even out the set, as if children were salt and pepper shakers, or socks, or collectable dolls.

Not long ago my baby-loving husband, who had been remarkably restrained during the first eighteen months of Micah's campaign to upend our home, asked, 'When are we going to have the next one?'

I looked at him sidelong, not surprised but discomfited. 'You remember what a pill I was when I was pregnant?' I said.

'Yes,' he said, sombrely. He remembered that noodle-eating harpy, shouting one moment and clinging to him in tears the next.

'You really want to invite that woman back into our house?'

'Yes.'

I know he doesn't actually want to deal with a pregnant woman again, or at least not this one—I really was a pain in the backside, although I will always maintain that I had every reason. But he wants another baby desperately, ideally would like two more, which I always tell him he is welcome to do with his second wife. He is one of those men who is great with babies, who is better at soothing and nurturing them than many women, and if he could strap on a womb for nine months he would happily oblige. As would I—why not share the experience, I don't need to monopolise it. I did not enjoy pregnancy and I dread the thought of going there again, even while acknowledging what a privilege it is and how lucky I will be to carry a second child to term at my, um, advancing age. Any pregnancy I manage now will be officially 'geriatric' according to the medical fraternity. Charming. Way to sugar-coat it, guys.

Next time around, if we are so blessed, I will at least know what to expect. I will not be surprised every week like I was last time, as some new, unexpected and often unsettling thing happened to my body. I will experience fewer disappointments too, I imagine, as I already know that maternity jeans are not all they are promised to be, and that feeling baby movements, while amazing, is less awe-inspiring at 3 am, which is to say that I am not the patient and accepting expectant mama I had hoped I would be.

People have stopped asking when we are going to give Micah a sibling, probably because they didn't get a particularly encouraging response from me in the past. I don't care to discuss family planning with any but my closest friends and relations. For one thing, I am unsure how I feel about having another child, and don't want to have to articulate that with someone I don't know particularly well. Secondly, I may not be able to. I didn't have trouble getting pregnant before, but time has passed, I have dropped from one age group category to another, and my chances of falling pregnant have diminished, quite naturally and appropriately. In her early thirties a woman has a fifteen per cent chance of getting pregnant each month. That falls to ten per cent when she is 35-plus and five per cent at 40. The cold hard truth is a bitch.

Which means I have a sense of urgency about having another child while also dreading the anticipated illness, fatness, exhaustion and round-the-clock newborn care, not to mention integrating another kid into Micah's world, where even the beloved family dog is a source of jealousy. If Scout is sitting on a lap, Micah will push his way past, squeezing himself between dog and parent—not because he doesn't adore 'Guy-guy' but because he wants to be top banana. If we scold him for being mean to Scout—extending a chubby hand to smack him, taking biscuits from his bowl and waving them around in a confusing manner, pulling his silky ears— Micah will scowl for a moment, an adorable thunder cloud, then give Scout a kiss on the flank and move in for 'a coddle' as Scout scuttles sideways, crab-like, and retreats to his den under our bed. Friends have told me about their first children bopping their second children on the head, moving them forcibly out of their way so they can get to the biscuits, turning hugs into anaconda death squeezes when parents look away, and I am sure Micah will react to a baby the same way. After all, he is a toddler and the world revolves around him.

Less expectedly, mothers of multiple children have told me they resented the arrival of a second child for fear it would strain their bond with the first. Babies divide and conquer families, thrusting themselves into the centre of any and all action, every decision, every event—even their big brother's car-themed birthday party or special rainy-day storybook-reading afternoon with Mummy. This can be hard for a mother who has been absorbed in loving her toddler for the past couple of years, even if she knows that, with time, she will feel the same way about the new baby.

And what of the environmental and geopolitical implications? If I am going to worry about this issue, I may as well do so on a global level. Do I really need to bring another resource-gobbling human being into this world? The planet is struggling to cope with the effects of those of us already here, charging around in our fossil-fuel devouring vehicles, casting off our detritus into landfills, pushing other species out of existence. And what sort of world are we gifting our children, anyway? Terrorists, fantasists, despots, greed-merchants, psychopaths, infomercial producers . . . Is this a place you would wish on an innocent? In my darkest moments, I wonder what we're thinking, submitting all these gorgeous babies to our madness.

The average New Zealand family is on the decline, according to Statistics New Zealand, as is the case in many other OECD countries. While we reliably produced four or more children per family in the 1800s, three children per family in the 1930s, and four children per family in the 1960s, we are barely making replacement rate now, despite a mini baby-boom in the last decade. There were 64,343 live births in New Zealand in 2008, the most since 1971. Our most fertile year, according to records, was 1961, when we produced 65,390 babies. It is worth noting that some families continue to flourish and in fact, prop up the rest of us population-wise. Maori and Pacific Island families are larger than Pakeha and Asian families, with younger parents. The average Maori woman has 2.8 children, compared with the national average of 2.2.

But overall, the family is dwindling. According to Jo Cribb in the article 'Focus on Families: New Zealand Families of Yesterday, Today and Tomorrow' published in the *Social Policy Journal of New Zealand*:

The number of children being born is decreasing (in actual numbers and as a proportion of the population) as more people stay single, more people partner but do not have children, and more women delay having children until they are financially settled—often in their mid 30s or later.

Despite this identified trend, as a culture we are not in favour of one-child families in New Zealand. We tend to look on only children with a sense of pity and mistrust, waiting for them to turn into precocious monsters with embarrassingly large vocabularies and entitlement complexes. We're not just being unkind. Research has found that children with siblings have better social skills than only children, are more attuned to others' feelings, and are better at making friends and helping others. Having been raised as an only child, with four older half-siblings in another country, I would not want that for my own son. I was a 'lonely only', not one of those kids who relish being the centre of their parents' world, although I was lavished with attention and that had obvious benefits. I wanted to share my peripatetic childhood with someone my own age, an ally. I behaved like a little adult far too soon, and clearly remember creating imaginary siblings to play with, which seems tragic now although at least they were 70s chic: one of the little boys had a bowl haircut and cowboy boots. It would be nice now, too, to have a sibling with whom to share childhood memories.

A friend mused that there seems to be a trend towards three-child families in middle-class New Zealand with the annoying undertone that if you can manage three children it is because you are a particularly well-organised, competent mother, *and* you can afford it, meaning children are becoming a status symbol in the same way that iPhones and the latest road-biking gear are status symbols. Certainly I struggle to see how my husband and I could afford to provide for three children on one-and-a-half salaries, even when you factor in the economies of scale to be had from hand-me-down clothes and furniture, books and toys—not if we planned to send the kids to enrichment activities, like swimming lessons, art workshops, pony club and goodness knows what else. Of course it's possible for many families, but without killing ourselves working to fulfil the heightened expectations as to what children should be doing with their time, I can't see it working for us. It would seem to be making the already challenging task of running a family that much more challenging.

In the United States, there is an identified move towards larger families among middle-class and wealthy professionals. While nationally the US is seeing a decline in fertility (like the rest of the Western world), there are pockets of resistance, where families are bucking the trend. In the plush suburbs of the San Francisco Peninsula, where four-child families are fashionable, people say 'three is the new two', according to *San Francisco* magazine. They even have a name for them: Woodside Four, after the affluent suburb of Woodside that's filled with Silicon Valley executives and lawyers. Among Woodside Four families it is considered a privilege to be able to afford an upper middle-class lifestyle with all the bells and whistles (sports cars, boats, skiing chalets, electronic gizmos, designer dogs) at the same time as raising a large family. Giving up on creature comforts *Swiss Family Robinson*-style is not something they need to consider.

The anecdotal evidence goes that even those affluent mothers who start later in life will not let a slowing biological clock deter them from their plans, and there is academic evidence to back that up. Sociologist Steve Martin from the University of Maryland found that university-educated women who put off motherhood until their 30s had children at an accelerated rate, and ended up with families almost as large as their peers who started at an earlier age. For these women, where there is a will and a big enough bank account, there is a way.

In Auckland, the three-child family boom appears to be centred around Pt Chevalier, Grey Lynn, Ponsonby and Western Springs. I met a mother-of-three at a summer barbecue heaving with fashionably attired poppets who told me the multiple-child family wasn't a status symbol in her set so much as a comment on job performance. For smart, educated women who have left successful careers to raise children, it can feel that the next logical step after successfully hatching two children and beginning the round of baby swimming lessons and tiny tots soccer and morning preschool sessions is to have a third baby. Success begets success.

'It's not about having money,' she laughed. 'If it was about having money my husband and I would never have had a third.'

How many is right for you? Everyone is different; Nicola, mother of two, says:

Two is so much harder than one.

Heather, mother of three, says:

Two is no worse than one. It's when you get to three
that you notice.

Assuming my fertility is not hopelessly withered now that I
am closer to 40 than 30, I look forward to seeing what kind
of big brother Micah will be, partly because he is such an
interesting little person, and a loving person. He is going
through a kissy phase now—he'll move around the room
kissing Mummy and Daddy, the dog, Teddy, Giraffe, and if
he is feeling particularly at peace with the world he will kiss
inanimate objects too: the sofa, the deck railing, a bench. He
has a fetish for shoes, liking to pair them and line them up
in his bedroom. Train slippers next to brown sandals next
to grey-and-red skate shoes next to gumboots next to alien-
and-flying-saucer slip-ons. When you try to push his feet
into shoes that are not in favour that day he gets *so* ticked off:
'Nooo! No. No. No,' he shouts while waving his arms and
kicking. He has, for no reason that we can find, developed an
obsession for modes of transport—cars especially, but trucks,
trains, planes, boats. This is in a one-car family, where neither
of us remembers to check the oil until the little red light comes
on. We're not car people and yet our son is a car man, passionately so. When the rubbish truck passes, he is thrilled to the
soles of his impeccably shod feet.

While I am sure Micah would be resistant to the idea of

sharing his parents with anybody, I think he would be fascinated by a baby's activities and eager to help fulfil a sibling's needs. He loves to help, bringing fresh towels to the newly showered, digging holes in the garden with Daddy, pulling the frying pan out of the drawer when Mummy is making fried eggs with bacon. With a baby I anticipate he would be a useful little runner, fetching nappies and wipes and toys.

This is an appealing vision, and yet I remain reluctant. It has taken until just before Micah's second birthday for me to feel like 'me' again. I am healthier, happier and more optimistic than I have been since I fell pregnant. I laugh more readily and I can finally fit into pants from my pre-child life. There is much to dread about incorporating another child into the family, while acknowledging that there are many joys to be anticipated as well: the privilege of having a tiny newborn in the house again, the expanded sense of family and love, the horizons newly visible.

If you are unsure about whether to have another child, I think it comes down to your gut feeling. You can weigh pros and cons and calculate household income versus expenditure, even borrow someone else's baby for a night or two as a dry run, but you will have a sense, a knowing tucked away deep inside, about what is the right choice for you and yours. Will you hit menopause and regret not having tried for another child? Do you think your child needs a sibling? Does your partner desperately want another? Can you handle another pregnancy and birth?

I finally realised I was ready to add another baby to our family when we took Micah and his cousin Reuben to a seaside playground one afternoon late in summer when Auckland was hot as the Devil's breath and the water beckoned. As we drove, the two little boys sat in their car seats holding hands and giggling, conspiring wordlessly. A mere look from one would set the other off in fits of laughter. When we arrived at the playground they separated to do their own thing: the slide for Micah, the jiggly car for Reuben. But when the Mr Whippy van turned up they were again united in purpose. Which ice cream did they want? The choc dip. Two, please. They sat side by side on a little rock wall and pulled pieces of chocolate shell off their ice creams, licking vanilla rivers off their arms, asking for their hands to be wiped. They were so cute passersby couldn't resist admiring them, and I melted too. I thought: chubby little humans. Two, please.

But I have plenty of cautionary tales to keep me sober. Mother of two Maria found it difficult to cope with a new baby and a toddler:

> The first weeks at home with the first baby were wonderful, the second time round it was hell. My two-year-old kept hitting the baby and I was desperately tired. We had a student in to cook and help out for a couple of weeks as I'd had a caesarian and had no in-laws around to assist and the girls' dad was working. The day my helper left I was distraught; she made me feel so cared for. I wanted to cling to her legs and beg her not to go.

Heather said her easygoing second child lulled her into having a third, who was fussy and unsettled and wouldn't sleep. Gillian found the same with her second daughter, who paved the way for a firebrand third.

I have a friend who tells me she always knew being a mother would be her special talent, the one thing on this earth that she was meant to do, and the evidence is there for all to see. She is brilliant at it, her three children are gorgeous and polite and caring and sharp as tacks, and in a real sign of talent, people look to my friend for guidance on how to make their own families work better. I do not share her certainty about the mothering role. I love aspects of motherhood. I adore my boy, and would never want to be without him. But I am still me, and while I don't (usually) resent putting Micah first at all times and in all situations, sometimes, honestly, I struggle with it a little, because I have dreams that do not relate to motherhood and are difficult to marry with my life now. I realise that even mentioning that is risky, because mothers are not supposed to admit that they want anything else in this world than happy, healthy children. But I do.

A lot of mothers do struggle to manage two or more small children, and plans for career advancement often fall by the wayside at this point in a woman's life. She may find that returning to work does not feel like the best use of her time, or that having taken a break to have more children, she has been left behind in a competitive field. Still others find that the more children they have the happier their home life becomes and the more fulfilled they feel. You can't really know until you do it, same as your first child. Deciding whether to have a second (or third or fourth) child is kind of like getting married, or moving in with someone, or buying a house, or moving to a new country. By all means do the research, so you are making an informed choice, but ultimately you have to give in to your heart and hope for the best.

Further reading

The New Zealand Family from 1840: A Demographic History, by Ian Pool, Arunchulam Dharmalingam, and Janet Sceats, Auckland University Press, 2007

'New Zealand Women Stop Having Babies', *Sunday Star-Times*, 30 March 2008

'The Woodside Four: Got Baby? With the Peninsula's Smart Set, Four's the Magic Number' by Leslie Gordon, *San Francisco Magazine*, August 2005

'Family Size in America: Are Large Families Back?' at babycenter.com

13. The cherry on top
The extra bits

Now that I am a mother, I am all for keeping things simple, and that is the reasoning behind this final chapter. You may not have the time or energy to read an entire book on navigating new motherhood. I understand, and I will not be at all offended if you prefer this distilled version. Enjoy!

Mothering wisdom

1. Pregnancy is wondrous, but not always fun. It is actually okay to say you're having a lousy day—I give you permission. Remember, there is always someone out there who was a less beatific pregnant woman than you, and that woman is probably me.

2. People will offer you a lot of advice, most of which you will not want. Smile and nod and if they are *really* getting

on your nerves, think of puppies or French perfume or chocolate birthday cake. Or tell them to take a flying leap—they'll probably blame it on the hormones and sleepless nights anyway.

3. The first weeks at home with a new baby are a crazy whirlwind. Be kind to yourself. If you accomplish two non-baby related tasks a day, give yourself a pat on the back. You are amazing!

4. Don't panic if you feel that your identity has been stolen in the night and you are forever going to be solely known as someone's mummy. You will return to yourself. It may take a couple of years, but it will happen.

5. Making mummy friends can be surprisingly difficult if you prefer to maintain your pre-child personality. If you find the coffee group thing unappealing, you are not alone. Call me.

6. Your sleep is going to be disrupted. This is exceedingly unpleasant, but part and parcel of parenting. It is a major reason why 24 year olds make perkier new mummies than 34 year olds. Also why many new dads scuttle off to the spare room for a few months.

7. The so-called mummy wars do not exist. Neither does the supermum. So there, stop worrying about them. Doesn't that feel better?

8. We over-think parenting in the twenty-first century. We all need to take a deep breath and remember that we, as children, did not benefit from baby Mandarin lessons or under-two's soccer and we turned out fine. Our babies will, too.

9. Other mothers are not going to agree with you about immunisation, working outside the home, family size, baby names, disposable nappies, home births and a thousand other topics. That is okay. Do your own thing. If the über-mummies at daycare shun you for using formula that's their problem, not yours.

10. Your partner is going to manage the baby differently from you do, and their methods may even look a tad dangerous to your mother-hawk eyes. Instead of having an argument about the correct way to use a Jolly Jumper, leave them to it, and go lie down. Better yet, lie down with a good book, some baked naughtiness and a glass of something relaxing.

Mothering secrets

* I dyed my hair while pregnant. Not in the first trimester, I would point out, and only after reading in my worry-wart's handbook, *Pregnancy Dos and Don'ts: The Smart Woman's A–Z Pocket Companion for a Safe and Sound Pregnancy* by Dr Elisabeth Aron, that hair dye had not been associated with any adverse foetal outcomes. It did not hurt my baby and I felt 1000 per cent better about myself once I got rid of my muddy roots.

* I ate a piece of sushi in my third trimester. Everyone survived and it tasted like heaven.

* To stave off nausea I ate five meals a day. Unfortunately, two of them were devoid of nutritional value because I had to have my instant noodles and my sour cream-flavoured rice crackers. I did, however, take a good pre-natal vitamin and was religious with the folic acid.

* Vitamin A and E oil applied all over every day, with special attention paid to my stomach, helped me feel pretty while pregnant. In possibly related news, I did not get stretch marks.

* You do not need any specialised maternity clothes other than a black stretchy skirt, a long stretchy singlet and a pair of preggo-lady leggings. I got mine from a maternity boutique and they were worth every cent because I thrashed them and even wore the preggo leggings for a year after giving birth. You do, however, need good maternity bras.

* I exercised throughout my pregnancy with help from my personal-trainer friend and nothing bad happened. In fact, I felt much better for it mentally and I am convinced it helped me recover from the birth faster. We did a gentler form of my pre-pregnancy workout, and made sure I didn't get too hot.

* Baby wipes are incredibly useful. I carry them around with me all the time now, for when I need to clean my hands after putting on make-up in the car, or when I need to quickly polish my shoes, or get dried food off my clothes, or give the kitchen bench a cheat's wipe before someone pops round. Do not buy the cheapest brand— like the cheapest nappies, these are inferior in quality and you will need three to do the job of one of the decent ones.

* Capsules are the best thing ever invented for newborn care. You can't leave your baby in the capsule all the time, of course, but when you are going from car to shops to car to home, they make life so much easier. If you don't want

to invest in one, Plunket has a great car seat rental scheme. If you get a capsule, make sure you also get the 'snap 'n' go' wheels and base, so you can turn it into a pram. Baby need not wake while this happens. Genius!

* Babies love to play with wrapping. You may have already heard this, but seriously, it is the cheapest toy in Christendom, next to an empty toilet roll. For the first Christmas and birthday, don't go overboard on pressies but make sure you wrap everything in glitzy, glittery disco paper so your little one can scrunch it between their fingers, wave it over their heads, and roll around in it like a calf in clover.

* The best beauty product for the new mother is blusher. It will help you fake the glow everyone expects you to be exuding. The other essential cosmetic item for helping you look on top of things is mascara, which makes your eyes look wide awake even when they're not.

* Some shopping areas and malls have special parking spots for parents of small children. I did not notice these until Micah was eighteen months old and I had already perfected my car park-pram shuffle. But next time I have a littlie, I'm so there.

* Teething is a painful time for babies and parents. After trying teething gel, rusks, chew toys, and chew toys that you pop in the freezer, I discovered teething powder. I would dunk Micah's dummy in the pottle and he would immediately calm down. Even seeing the pottle made him feel better.

* Unless you want to become a children's music aficionado, don't play it in the car, because down that road lies several

miserable years of Baby Dub and Putamayo. Sprogs will quite happily listen to your music (obviously, the stuff with child-friendly lyrics), and will clap their hands and ask for more. Even when they discover kids' music at music class or preschool they won't expect to hear it in the car if you have conditioned them to expect U2.

Wish fulfilment
What mothers really want

As part of the research for this book, I asked the question, 'What would make the job of mothering easier?' The answers were varied:

Support is the biggest thing. The trick is finding helpful and useful support. Someone who can actually be there without evoking any sense of guilt for the state of the house, the state of me, or for me wanting to have some time without my darling child. My sister once sent me an alphabet of mothering and I remember G was 'Guilt is to mothering like rain is to somewhere in America'— get used to it, it is the normal condition!—Anneliese, mother of three

More money!—Belinda, mother of one

Having the role of motherhood truly accepted in the workforce. For mothers and fathers to be treated equally at work. A mother who takes time off to look after a sick child or go to a sports day or a doctor's appointment is seen as if she's not taking her job seriously, while a man who does the same is a 'good, hands-on father'. I'm sure you know what I mean. And for people to be a bit more considerate when parking their cars (or wheelie bins) in the middle of the footpath, so I have to take my precious offspring onto the busy road to get around them.—Lee-Anne, mother of two

Having someone to come in and clean the house, maybe even twice a week.—Nicola, mother of two

Maybe a user's manual.—Diana, mother of one

People don't tell you how hard motherhood is—the reality of it—and you're not supposed to talk about it. But we should.—Caroline, mother of two

Mrs Incredible's stretchy super powers! And the ability to mute/pause children with the push of a button! Seriously, helpful relatives nearby and a live-in housekeeper who is just like part of the family, but fades away so you can have family time. Okay . . . I'm dreaming again. I always feel much better about parenting when my parents stay with us. I think it's the relentlessness again. But I don't want to hire a nanny. I like being a 'hands-on' mother most of the time. I am happy working part-time. I just wish I didn't have to do housework.—Kaila, mother of three

A better healthcare system in this country. This is part of the reason we are not having number two.—Sonia, mother of one

I think mothering would be a whole lot easier if people lived in the same place as their families. Better part-time work options. More value placed on the job stay-at-home parents do.—Rebecca, mother of two

A cook and a cleaner. I don't want to spend any less time with my kids, I just don't want to deal with any of the other household stuff.—Sharon, mother of two

A full time cleaner, fully paid salary for at least the first year, someone to force you every week to take one hour out just for yourself.—Vanessa, mother of two

Having a set day when we said we were just going to play with the kids and not do any other work.—Helen, mother of two

In practical terms, I think some financial contribution by the government for stay-at-home mums would definitely help. As currently they'll pay for my child to go into daycare, but won't pay me a cent to look after my child. Just so there is some acknowledgement of the value of the job we do in contributing to society, and so I can make some (no matter how little) contribution to the family income.—Anna, mother of two

Having a really good support network, for me that is one of the reasons I probably ended up with postnatal depression. I didn't have those support networks and felt really isolated. And making sure that you have time out on a regular basis. More sleep!—Heather, mother of three

New mothers need more information to help them after the birth. Other than that, I really have no idea what would make mothering easier. By definition it's just difficult, although very rewarding.—Angela, mother of one

People keeping their opinions to themselves when advice is not asked for unless it's helpful advice, also people not comparing their children with yours and making you feel like your baby is not as advanced or as good as theirs.—Nikki, mother of two

Oh I didn't expect that

Again, when I asked 'What surprised you most about motherhood?' the answers were mostly positive:

I had never liked kids particularly, plus I assumed I wouldn't be able to have them. I still look at my kids in total wonder. I can't believe that unconditional love, that I enjoy being with them so much, and that they are now bigger than me.—Maria, mother of two

The fact that your heart really is worn outside your body. The fact that you always have to be the adult. The fact that you can never ever stop being a parent for one minute of any day, ever.—Jo, mother of one

How much fun it is! We love having our kids around, they are hilarious and great company. We have so much fun together. I can't believe the people we come across who almost treat being parents as a job; a chore. They can't wait to get away from their kids and are never happier than when they're dumping them on someone else, or going on holiday without them so they can have a break. I think that's so sad as they rob themselves and their kids of some wonderful experiences. We hate being away from our boys!—Jackie, mother of two

The amount of love, and the compromises I am willing to make for my children.—Gillian, mother of three

I thought I was a bit of a failure, having succeeded at most things in life that I had put my mind to, but with mothering I had no way of knowing whether or not I was doing the right thing.—Kylie, mother of two

How much I adore it and my lovely child. She is such a gift, in so many ways, a great travel companion, a raconteur and a talented beauty!—Linda, mother of one

I admire my son. I knew I would love him, but I admire his character. He is very loving and empathetic.—Steph, mother of one

Hard-won truths

Here is the best mothering advice gleaned from my research:

It's as hard as you make it. If you stay calm and stop second-guessing yourself you'll be amazed at what you can achieve. Oh and most men, as hard as they try, really are quite useless. But as a mother you have to learn to keep your trap shut and let them have a go—otherwise they will never help again.—Maree, mother of two

Pick your battles.—Alice, mother of two

Babies don't follow the rules in the book, just go with the flow. If your baby is happy and active you are doing a good job no matter what the state of the house is, so just enjoy them.—Gillian, mother of three

Don't feel the pressure to breastfeed if it's not for you. Don't feel guilty about your c-section if your child's head is enormous and would never have come out any other way.—Linda, mother of one

Don't worry about other priorities which with hind-sight will seem irrelevant. I remember when I had to take time off if a child was sick and worrying about having to cancel a work meeting, or bringing a report home to try and work on it in between tending to a sick child, but when I look back, I wonder why I bothered as those priorities seem so inconsequential years later.—Fiona, mother of two

Modern kids eat all kinds of food like sushi that I never had growing up if you feed it to them early!—Joanna, mother of two

The best advice I got—no baby has ever died from crying. The best advice I can impart—sleep with earplugs, otherwise every single gurgle, snort, fart and murmur will have you sitting bolt upright ready to leap out of bed. Oh and if you don't have to, don't sleep them in your bedroom. Having them in the room just means dads get shitty nights' sleep, too, and unless you like sharing the pain and the hurt, I would prefer to have a happy husband than a tired, crabby one.—Maree, mother of two

People told me time goes fast, don't miss a moment, but I didn't realise and I wish I had.—Sophie, mother of one

Guinness is really good for breast milk. Seriously, ride it. Go with it. Don't fight it.—Sarah, mother of two

You can't worry about what other people say. You have to do what is right for you; their opinion doesn't really matter.—Tracey, mother of two

My best advice? Don't listen to me or anyone else. Mother how you want to, so long as there's plenty of love.—Steph, mother of one

So, was it worth it and would I do it again? Unequivocally, yes. Motherhood for me is a joy and an honour and, there's no doubt about it, an almighty challenge—my personal Everest, I suspect. It has opened me up to a new set of people and experiences. It has brought me closer to family and friends. It has also taught me a lot about empathy and patience, and that, too, is a gift. Both Tim and I have found the ups and downs of life with our little man hilarious, confounding, heart-expanding, and inspiring. It just keeps getting better. What more could you ask for?

Further reading

If you liked this book, you'll love these:

Everybody into the Pool: True Tales by Beth Lisick, Regan Books, 2005. It's not a parenting book but a very funny memoir about a woman who has a baby while living in 'Brokeley', the urban smear where Berkeley and Oakland, California, merge. The houses are gorgeous old Craftsmen-style places, bungalows and Victorians, but the area is not much better than a slum. Beth is a performance artist and writer with a finely tuned sense of the ridiculous. She is one of my heroes.

The Slippery Year: A Meditation on Happily Ever After by Melanie Gideon, Orion, 2001. Again, not a parenting book (sense a theme here?) but a smart exploration of the emptiness that can creep into the mothering life, and indeed the life of any middle-class woman, parent or not. She says, 'I am one of the millions who is currently walking around in a daze, no longer recognising herself, wondering *Is this all there is?*'

The Fish Finger Years: What Your Mother Never Told You About Bringing Up Kids by Fiona Gibson, Hodder & Stoughton Ltd, 2005. She grabbed my attention by saying raising children is like raising tiny drunks, and she kept it by sharing her tales of the year she tried to palm off carob Easter treats on her boys, and by insisting that 'staying in is the new going out'. I kind of wish she lived around the corner from me.

Mommies Who Drink: Sex, Drugs and Other Distant Memories of an Ordinary Mom by Brett Paesel, Warner Books, 2006. Worth mentioning again because it is so funny and so real, even though it's set in Los Angeles. I particularly love the part where Brett goes to a coffee group afternoon and gets so bored she steals a lipstick, not that I would ever sanction that sort of behaviour, but I do understand her desperation.

Operating Instructions: A Journal of My Son's First Year by Anne Lamott, Pantheon, 1993. A wonderful book from a wonderful writer and, I would surmise, a wonderful mother. Struggling to cope with raising a baby son on her own, she wrote her days into a diary that became this book. It is as warm and inviting as a snuggly blanket.

Acknowledgements

Thanks to the lovely Allen & Unwin team: Siobhán Cantrill, Fiona McRae, Josie Brennan, Abba Renshaw—and especially Nicola McCloy.

Special thanks to the fifty wonderful women who took the time to answer my questions with such honesty and good humour.

And, to my family and friends, who put up with me through it all—much love.